TWO CAN PLAY

By Jamaica's most outstanding playwright

Trevor Rhone

Introduction by MICHAEL MANLEY
Prime Minister of Jamaica
1972 to 1980

KET BOOKS EDITION

The special television performance of *Two Can Play,* starring Grace
McGhie and Charles Hyatt is available for broadcast on one-inch Type
C video tape, or for home use on 1/2″ VHS or Beta formats.

ISBN 0-910475-27-X

Also by Trevor Rhone

Old Story Time and other plays

Published by Longman House
Burnt Mill, Harlow, Essex, UK

Films
The Harder They Come
Smile Orange

When Trevor Rhone wrote *Smile Orange* and *School's Out*, his first major plays, it was immediately obvious a real dramatic talent had arrived on the Jamaican scene. His ear for dialogue, his eye for characterization, and his feel for situation set him apart as a true craftsman.

These uncompromising powers of observation — together with Rhone's economy of language — also suggested the success of his first offerings would be no mere "flash in the pan." A play, after all, must hold its audience, tell its story, and convey its message almost exclusively through speech. A play cannot be rescued by arresting passages of descriptive prose; nor can it use simple narrative to explore the interior landscape of private emotion. These mechanisms are open to the novelist, but virtually closed to the playwright. A dramatist without an ear for dialogue is like a sniper without a scope for his rifle: still potentially powerful and threatening, but limited in his range and largely ineffective.

And yet, if conversational dialogue is the main weapon in the playwright's armoury, it follows that with his plays he must take aim at the complexities of human interaction. Consequently, most theatre of the non-escapist kind resolves itself, at last, into social commentary.

Social commentary, itself, may take many forms. It may reflect the surface of things as a photograph does; or it may probe the causes of the things it sees. It may be optimistic, spotlighting changes for the better; or it may be pessimistic, demonstrating yet again that the more things change the more they remain the same. So too may the dramatist-as-commentator be considered a "photographer" or a "prober"; and, concurrently, an optimist or a pessimist.

In the same vein, the dramatist may be further categorized as an idealist, a sentimentalist, a cynic, or a realist. The idealist tends to distort reality as he makes his case for human perfectability. The sentimentalist ignores reality altogether. Neither label has any place in this discussion, for Trevor

Rhone is too uncompromisingly rooted in the everyday realities to be classed as an idealist or a mystic. Nor can he ever be dismissed as a sentimentalist.

Quite the contrary: It was the powerful realism of Rhone's first two works that validated his claim as a theatrical force to be reckoned with. Unfortunately, that reckoning had to be postponed. Both *Smile Orange* and *School's Out* were more photographic than probing. Both works reflected a bleak view of human nature, but the question mark remained: Were the formidable talents displayed on stage mere furniture from the dwelling place of a cynic?

The dividing line between cynicism and realism is difficult to locate. Indeed, the cynic will tell you it is an imaginary line — that any "realistic" view of the human condition must be "cynical." The distinction is important, however, in art; and nowhere more important than in literature and drama.

To the cynical artist, "human development" is a contradiction in terms. To his mind human relationships are superficial, consisting only of a kind of sparring between equally self-absorbed participants. He believes human beings are driven by base motives to sordid activities. There are no solutions. There is not even the possibility of personal growth.

The realist sees what the cynic sees, and knows much of it is true. But he also sees what the cynic does not see: There can be more to life than sordid activity. People can (and do) change and develop. Moreover, the realist understands it is only when people are deprived of their aspirations and their development that life becomes an unendurable humbug.

It was with his third play, *Old Story Time*, that Trevor Rhone showed himself to be a realist in the finest sense of the term. Therein he demonstrated his comprehension of both the limitations and the possibilities of the human condition. The furniture of dramatic skills was displayed again, even more highly polished than before. And there was much more. The play probed, but lovingly. Its characters engaged our sympathy, even as they claimed our recognition. Regions of the heart were explored —regions where cynics dare not tread.

Now we have *Two Can Play*: Trevor Rhone's second masterpiece of dramatic realism.

Two Can Play is set in a house in Rollington Town: the home of a typical (indeed, prototypal) lower-middle-class couple —Gloria and Jim. The pair are the only on-stage characters in the play. Jim's father lies dying, offstage, during the first scene. Away in the United States of America are the couple's three children, smuggled into that country to "better themselves."

The first scene is played out to a background of M-16 rifle fire, as the General Election of 1980 unfolds its own particular brand of murder and mayhem. But it is soon clear to the audience that the gunfire is as incidental as the background music of a film. The play is about men and women, husbands and wives, and the socialization of the sexes.

Two Can Play is about love, and estrangement; about domination, and liberation; about confusion, and compassion. It is about two human beings who nearly lose one another — but who eventually struggle back together through uncertainty, through quarrels, through humiliation. Ultimately, Gloria and Jim survive because they learn to communicate and, finally, to re-discover one another — not so much as they were, but as what they each can try to become.

As in his earlier plays, Rhone's dialogue is compact, accurate, and telling. His characters often are funny — not because the playwright is reaching for comic effect, but because Trevor Rhone understands that humor is a survival mechanism for the working class.

Gloria and Jim are "fed up" with the situation in Rollington Town. So they work out a very complicated (and deliciously dishonest) scheme for getting permanent visas to the United States. This plot-within-a-plot calls for Gloria to "divorce" Jim and to "marry" a bona fide black U.S. citizen. Having thus acquired her own visa, she is to then "divorce" her new husband and "remarry" Jim.

Unfortunately for Jim (fortunately for the audience), the break in the couple's chain of existence releases in Gloria a long pent-up need for self-discovery and personal development. When Gloria returns to Jamaica from her new "marriage," her need for liberation precipitates a crisis in the relationship — and the focus of the play. By now it is clear to the audience that both the situation in Rollington Town and the opportunity (real or imagined) for emmigration are mere incidents, no more central than stage props. The real struggle, as always, is within and between the two participants in this very human relationship.

The second act explores this trauma, with its despair and its confusion. Then comes the first glimmering of true understanding; and the final re-discovery of one another, on a new plane, has to stand as one of the most moving episodes in Jamaican drama. It elevates Trevor Rhone above the status of a good, or even brilliant, playwright — and suggests he may indeed be a great one. To his superb sense of characterization at the more obvious levels, he has added a deep and compassionate understanding of human need and aspiration.

The theme of domination is woven through all history and across all continents. Always, it is the use of force that establishes the peculiar relationship — the subjugation of people and peoples by other, more powerful groups. And always, whether it be soon or late, the dominated rise up to claim their freedom.

Woman, no less than any nation, has been subjugated and dominated throughout history. The colo female through marriage is as old as organi: woman, too, has come (albeit recently) to her freedom. Her struggle is by no means supposedly "most advanced" societies.

In *Two Can Play*, Trevor Rhone presen theme of domination and struggle in a d form. Jim, the husband, expects to be serve by his wife. Meanwhile, he is ignorant o expectations — he can not bring Gloria to no one thought to tell him how (or even t know). As such, Jim represents a prototype: may be found in Birmingham, Alabama England no less than in Kingston, Jamaic

Yet it is a credit to Trevor Rhone's talent t Gloria and Jim remain absolutely Jamaic down-town Kingston — while their pro universality. The play measures the diale between them, a process necessarily triggere journey of self-discovery.

Trevor Rhone's triumph lies in the fac credible an ending filled with the pr possibility — a possibility that transcends their house, the disappointments of Amerio of Jamaica, and the failures of their own

THE SETTING

The play is set in Kingston, Jamaica, in the late 1970's, in what was once a lower middle income area. The area has been ravaged by the effects of political warfare, and is now a deprived and depressed area, falling just short of being a ghetto.

The stage set is the interior of what was formerly a fairly decent looking house, with lattice work, inside bathrooms, etc. The house has become a prison, just as hard to get out of as it is to get into.

There are two main areas:

Area 1: The dining area, with kitchen off it. Part of the kitchen's counter and shelving are visible. There is a window which looks to the outside. The front door entrance to the house is visible. Both window and front door are secured by bolts, pins, and grillwork.

In the dining area there is the obligatory shelving which contains the family photographs, crochet doilies and other bric-a-brac.

Area 2: The main bedroom, with a bathroom off it. A window looks to the outside. It is secured by bolts and grillwork.

These two areas are linked by a corridor. One other bedroom door is visible on this corridor.

Central to the setting is the security grill gate, complete with chain, lock, and bolts. It separates the sleeping area from the rest of the house.

GLOSSARY

A	I, remains as 'I' when used for emphasis
ackee and saltfish	a Jamaican dish
Bellevue	the name of a mental asylum
blouse beat!	an expression of surprise
blue drawers	a Jamaican dish
bruck	broken
buss	burst
bwoy	boy
battyman	homosexual
cheups	a light affectionate kiss on the lips
coz	because
cuss	curse
dat	that
dem	them
dis	this
F.I.U.	Financial Intelligence Unit— a unit for policing the leakage of foreign exchange
gal	girl
ginny	jenny-ass, female donkey
hear dey	listen to that
mi	my
mi nuh 'fraid	I am not afraid
nutten	nothing
odder	other
out dey	out there, outside
pickney	child
Star	Jamaican evening newspaper
tief	steal
wid	with
yuh	your (when used as an adjective: e.g., "yuh head")
	you (when used as a pronoun: e.g., "where yuh going")

TREVOR RHONE'S **TWO CAN PLAY**
Act I, Scene i

[*Incidental reggae music continues over as the house lights go to black. The actors come on in the blackness. The stage lights come up slowly, as gun shots explode in the distance and dogs bark frantically. JIM and GLORIA are lying in bed.*]

JIM: Gloria?

GLORIA: Yes, Jim.

[*Gunshots, dogs barking*]

JIM: Hear dey ... is war out dey.

[*Gunshots getting louder*]

JIM: We under seige tonight, Gloria.

GLORIA: Go to sleep, Jim.

JIM: But Gloria — it getting closer.

GLORIA: Put a pillow over yuh head.

[*Barrage of loud gunshots*]

JIM: It gettin' closer still ... Listen ...

[*GLORIA gets up off the bed and goes to the bathroom.*]

JIM: Where yuh going? ... Gloria?

[*GLORIA returns with a glass of water. She gives it to him with a pill which she takes from a pillbox kept in the bed head.*]

GLORIA: Here.

JIM: Is what?

GLORIA: The valium.

JIM: A take four already.

GLORIA: Take another one.

JIM: Mi inside like a drug store.

GLORIA: Take it.

[*JIM takes the tablet, pops it into his mouth and washes it down with water.*]

GLORIA: Now, try and sleep.

[*They both lie back in the bed. For a moment there is silence. Then shots — very loud. JIM and GLORIA jump up and look at each other. GLORIA reaches underneath the bed for a bottle of water and a cutlass, and goes toward the grill gate, while JIM reaches for a slipper and heads for the clothes closet.*]

JIM: Dat can't do nutten 'gainst M-16 ...

GLORIA: Oh yes? Make them come — make them come.

JIM: Gloria, dem shootin' up the house — dem shootin' it up!

GLORIA: Is by the gully.

JIM: No — is right inside here.

[*There is a big blast of automatic gunfire.*]

JIM: We dead! We dead! Gloria, Gloria, we dead!

[*He hides himself in the clothes closet. The gunfire dies down. Slowly he comes out.*]

A could swear it was in the house. It sound like it was right in here. Oh mi God!

GLORIA: Hang on to yuh nerves ...

[*She puts her weapons down and then consoles JIM.*]

JIM: A can't take it, Gloria — A can't take it no more ...

GLORIA: Pull yuhself together ... don't make it get to yuh,

Jim, or yuh gone to Bellevue ...

JIM: Lord have mercy.

GLORIA: One day it muss be over. It can't go on forever.

JIM: Is months now Gloria; is months.

[*GLORIA hums and then sings a little song: "What a fellowship, what a joy divine, leaning on ..." etc.*]

Sister Glo, yuh not 'fraid?

GLORIA: No Jim, 'fraid for what?

[*Loud blast of gun*]

JIM: Hear dey ... that one sound like a cannon.

GLORIA: Them call that one the Grandfather.

JIM: Pops! Go check on him.

GLORIA: Him okay.

JIM: Poor ole man. What a way to spend yuh last days. Jesus, it hot. In here is like a furnace. Go for the fan and put it on.

GLORIA: Last month light bill don't pay yet. Open the window.

JIM: Yuh must be mad!

GLORIA: Jim, yuh have to fight fear. Open the window.

JIM: No Gloria.

GLORIA: Open it, Jim.

[*Jim walks tentatively toward the window.*]

JIM: Lord, I am opening dis window coz it hot and A can't sleep; so if a bullet come in and blow off mi head, den is thy will and A will see yuh on the odder side. In the event dat A open it and all dat come in is the cool breeze, den yuh will see me right here in the morning. Night Lord. Night Glo. Turn off the light.

[*JIM returns to bed.*]

GLORIA: Jim.

JIM: Is what?

GLORIA: Yuh leave the manure round the front?

JIM: What a time to ask me dat. Yuh really think dey would tief the shit?

GLORIA: It would surprise yuh if yuh wake up in the morning and don't see it?

JIM: No. Turn off the light.

[*Gloria flicks off the bedside lamp. They lie in the half light for a while.*]

Turn back on the light Gloria.

GLORIA: What now?

JIM: A can't sleep with the window open.

[*He goes across and locks it.*]

What's the time?

GLORIA: One o'clock.

JIM: That's all? Is hours before day break.

GLORIA: Try an sleep.

JIM: Sleep? Me can't sleep. When A go to work A will sleep. A jus' hate the night time, y'know Gloria. Five o'clock in the evening is panic time for me, y'know Gloria.

GLORIA: Try an relax. Come.

[*He wanders around restlessly.*]

If yuh wasn't so stubborn we would move out of dis

neighbourhood long ago.

JIM: No way.

GLORIA: Yuh don't have to play brave with me. A not yuh friends on the corner. A hear yuh wid dem all the time "Dem have to kill me — dem not making me move."

JIM: Gloria, we can't afford uptown house.

GLORIA: Say dat ...

JIM: I born in dis neighbourhood — mi friends in dis neighborhood. I am alright — me nuh 'fraid.

[*Shots*]

Lord ... Give me another valium. Mi mind dashing all over the place ... the situation here — Pops — the children ...

GLORIA: If yuh was to hear that the children okay, yuh would feel better?

JIM: Boy Gloria, A would give mi eyeball to hear dat.

GLORIA: A hear from Andrew. Him write.

JIM: Jesus Christ! What yuh saying to me! Him write? Yuh crazy woman? Gloria, what A tell dem when dem was leaving? Gloria ... what A tell dem? If A sick, don't write. If dem hear A dead, don't communicate. Don't phone. Yuh know why A tell dem dat?

GLORIA: Yes Jim.

JIM: So why the ass yuh encourage dem to disobey mi orders?

GLORIA: A never encourage them Jim.

JIM: Yuh never discourage dem either. Yuh notice them don't write to me. After all the trouble and the sacrifice to get them there. Yuh know them can trace that letter ...

GLORIA: Trace what!

JIM: Uncle Sam is a bitch. Him have satellite up in the sky can read the number on dis house. Any return address on the letter?

GLORIA: No Jim.

JIM: At least him have that much sense. Him sign him name?

GLORIA: Just Boogsie.

JIM: Oh ...

GLORIA: Jesus Christ man! Why yuh so paranoid?

JIM: Paranoid? A not paranoid; mi nerves on edge, that's all. Gloria, them is illegal immigrant. Them convert the one entry, one week visa to permanent. One mistake, one slip up, and they right back here. A tell them, go underground, get lost, don't give Uncle Sam a chance to catch you. What Andrew say? Him not in any trouble?

GLORIA: Him O.K.

JIM: Lord be praised!

GLORIA: And him see Paul ...

JIM: Him really see Paul?

GLORIA: They meet on the subway.

JIM: Mi boys riding subway. Them gone underground in truth. A can imagine how they feel when they meet each other.

GLORIA: They living together.

JIM: Bad move dat. If they catch one, they catch two ...

GLORIA: Paul have three job.

JIM: Three jobs. Lord have mercy. Three jobs. One for every year him never work out here.

[*He goes down on his knees.*]

God bless America — God bless America.

GLORIA: And Andrew going to school full time ...

JIM: God bless America.

GLORIA: Paul supporting him.

JIM: Paul mi boy, like father like son. Yuh don't resemble me for nutten. Sending yuh little brother to school. Ai mi children. A was right to send dem away. Gloria, don't A was right?

[*Long pause*]

I love them too, Gloria. We tried with them here. You know how we sacrificed to send Paul to high school. For what? To sit on the corner for three years and keep bad company. Is prayers why the police never shoot him down ...

[*Pause — silence.*]

GLORIA: Andrew say he miss home.

[*Sound of gun shots*]

JIM: Listen to that. Is that him miss?

GLORIA: Is America the guns come from.

JIM: Or Cuba. A don't know. All A know is, we talking about survival. What about Suzie? Any word?

[*Pause*]

GLORIA: No....

[*She cries.*]

JIM: Look don't start. A want to cry too. So don't cry. Trust in the Lord. Uncle Sam will see them go right.

GLORIA: They don't belong to Uncle Sam.

JIM: Suzie sensible. A talk to her before A put her on the plane.

GLORIA: Jim where she sleep that first night? She sixteen and we just abandon her so ...

JIM: A never abandon her.

GLORIA: Is what den? A still can't believe I allow yuh to send her away ...

JIM: Is because yuh don't know what was happening to her out here. Is the whorehouse A rescue her from one day.

GLORIA: Suzie?!!

JIM: Two bad gal down the road inveigle her. Pops get word of it, and A bring her home. She promise to look something better. And if she go to America and whore, is better if we don't see. Yuh don't feel so too?

GLORIA: My Suzie?

JIM: Face facts Gloria. She never had a chance in this environment.

GLORIA: Is not the environment fail her.

JIM: I give them more than I ever get. Them at least get some schooling. A did mi best and when man on earth has done his best, angels can do no better. I don't fail them. Paul have three job and Andrew going to school. All they would have if they was still here would be me, you, and frustration. We couldn't help them anymore. A know it hard but is life. First thing in the morning A will tell Pops the good news. Him going be so happy; the way him love him grandchildren. Andrew ask for him?

GLORIA: Yes.

JIM: A know man. Is him favourite from time.

GLORIA: The house so lonely and quiet without dem ...

JIM: Paul have three jobs and Andrew going to school ...

[*Beat — coughing*]

[*Pause*]

GLORIA: Is Pops coughing so?

[*JIM listens briefly. Then he dashes toward the old man's room. He quickly returns.*]

JIM: Get out the tablets.

[*JIM searches for and finds the key that opens the grill door. He opens it and exits toward the kitchen, as GLORIA continues to search for the pills. Sound of water bottle as it drops and breaks. Jim returns from kitchen with the water.*]

Careful if yuh go in the kitchen. Pop's water bottle drop from me and buss. Pass the tablets.

GLORIA: A can't find them.

JIM: How yuh mean?

GLORIA: Dem not in here.

JIM: Yuh check the bathroom?

GLORIA: Yes, but is here A keep them.

JIM: But is only last week A fill the prescription.

GLORIA: Is last week's date on dis.

[*He takes the pill bottle and examines it.*]

JIM: They couldn't finish already. A don't understand.

[*Labored coughing, increasing in intensity*]

Go stay with him. I will call a doctor.

GLORIA: Which doctor yuh getting to come here at dis hour? Dem don't even come in the day.

[*JIM picks up the directory, looking for a number.*]

TREVOR RHONE 11

JIM: Maybe him can treat him over the phone.

GLORIA: Is the tablets him need.

JIM: Then look for them. Jesus Christ! Answer the phone man ... Hello — Doctor? Emergency! Mi father on dying ... Rollington Town area ... Yes, I can understand that, but the man is dying. Him swell up, hand, foot, everything .... Yes, him have a history of high blood pressure .... Ah, 72 next month ... yes ... yes, Doctor ... DIGO, X,l,N. Somehow it finish.

[*Intense coughing and gasping*]

GLORIA: Him coughing blood, Jim.

JIM: Him coughing blood now, Doctor ....

GLORIA: And froth, plenty, white looking stuff.

JIM: And froth, plenty, white looking stuff ... What is your address Doctor?

[*JIM grabs a pencil by the phone — he writes.*]

Eleven Tulip Drive, Norbrook ...

[*JIM hangs up the phone and turns to GLORIA.*]

GLORIA: What him say?

JIM: Him have some of the tablets at him house. If we want we can come for them.

GLORIA: Is 1:30 in the morning, taxi not coming down here.

JIM: Yuh think him can hold out till daylight?

GLORIA: Bwoy Jim, A don't think ... and anyway, we can't take dat chance ...

JIM: Rass!!

[*POPS coughs — gunshots — they look at each other.*]

GLORIA: Yuh might go out and ... Oh Jesus, what a life! You have to try an get them Jim, somehow.

JIM: But Gloria ...

GLORIA: If you can get out by the main, chances are yuh might pick up a taxi.

JIM: Yes. Yes.

[*Starts to dress*]

You got today, yesterday *Star?*

GLORIA: Here.

JIM: As A thought.

GLORIA: What?

JIM: Curfew.

GLORIA: No matter. Yuh have to try and get through. Is a matter of life or death.

JIM: But is war outside, Gloria.

GLORIA: No Jim, dat is madness. Even in war the wounded get a chance to get treatment.

[*JIM opens a window and looks out.*]

JIM: Rass!

GLORIA: What's the doctor's address?

[*She takes some clothes from the closet and she too starts to dress.*]

JIM: What yuh doin? Where yuh going?

GLORIA: One of us have to go Jim.

JIM: But Gloria, yuh might go out an' man rape yuh, gun yuh down.

GLORIA: A have to take dat chance.

JIM: The valium have me groggy ...

GLORIA: Is O.K. Yuh stay and look after him. Hot some water and clean him up.

JIM: Light the stove for me nuh.

[*GLORIA looks at him with a mixture of disgust and bitterness, annoyed at his ineffectualness. She then exits toward the kitchen, cursing him under her breath. Sound of GLORIA falling. She speaks from offstage.*]

GLORIA: Jesus! Oh Lawd! Aieeee ...

JIM: Gloria! What happen?

[*He crosses to the kitchen.*]

GLORIA: Is yuh buss the water bottle in here?

JIM: A did tell yuh ...

GLORIA: Why yuh never clean it up?

JIM: A was rushing. Yuh O.K.?

GLORIA: A think A buss mi hip ...

JIM: Come, let me help yuh inside.

[*As he helps her to the dining area, coughing is heard offstage.*]

GLORIA: Me okay. Pops!!

[*He leaves her and goes toward the bedroom to finish dressing, as she shuffles to the door and starts pulling the bolts. On the third bolt, the church bell tolls. As the lights dim, they both freeze momentarily. Then GLORIA sings a sad mournful song as JIM dresses for the funeral. He exits through POPS' room. GLORIA changes the tablecloth to a white one. Then she leaves for the bedroom. Still singing, she drapes the mirror with a black cloth, also ties her head with black material. Having done so she returns to the*]

*dining table to sit on the down right chair. The tolling
continues over till she sits and rests her head on the table,
eyes closed.*]

Act I, Scene ii

[*The lights go up to full on GLORIA, her head resting on the table, her eyes closed. It is evening, about 8:00, five days later. JIM enters through the front door. He is dressed in a muddied black suit, with his tie slightly askew.*]

JIM: Sister Glo, Sister Glo ...

[*She speaks as she wakes.*]

GLORIA: Yuh come?

JIM: Hm, how yuh feeling?

GLORIA: Nuh bad. How it went?

JIM: Aye Glo ...

GLORIA: What happen?

JIM: Is what never happen. Let me change dem clothes ...

[*He moves toward the bedroom.*]

GLORIA: Lawd God, how yuh dirty up so Jim?

JIM: Is a long story Glo.

[*He tries to walk away.*]

Oooh ...

[*He holds his back*].

GLORIA: What happen to yuh back? Yuh hurt yuhself?

JIM: Put it dis way — we both is invalids tonight; none to help the other. Oh, Lawd!

[*GLORIA struggles across to help him take off his jacket.*]

GLORIA: What happen?

[*She removes the jacket.*]

JIM: Glo, I give mi heart to dis country. A love the place. I am a good citizen; I pay mi taxes, A don't have any choice. A pay mi Housing Trust, although A don't have any benefit to get. I give mi sweat, mi tears, mi love. A had to send away mi children. What more dey want? Mi blood?

GLORIA: What happen Jim?

JIM: Wherever him is now, him happy. Him is out of dis misery. Walk good, Pops, walk good. Take care o'yuhself.

[*He cries*]

GLORIA: Is alright, is alright.

[*She reaches out to him.*]

How yuh hurt yuhself?

JIM: Them let go the coffin on me ...

GLORIA: How yuh mean?

JIM: When the shoot-out start.

GLORIA: Shoot-out? What shoot-out?

JIM: One shoot-out by the graveside today! One shoot-out! A pick the wrong day to bury the old man. Remember the whole heap o'gunfire the night Pops take in sick?

GLORIA: Yes ...

JIM: It was political warfare. One high-ranking capitalist gun man dead the night ...

GLORIA: And is today them decide to bury him ...

JIM: With full honours. Twenty-one gun salute ... right side where Pops suppose to bury.

GLORIA: Lord ha' mercy!

JIM: In the middle of the twenty-one gun salute, the socialist faction arrive ...

GLORIA: I can see it; don't tell me any more!

JIM: Them say the dead not buryin', coz the cemetery is in dem territory. And is den the gun battle really start. On the first volley, the pall bearers who carrying Pops drop the coffin and take foot for it. Them let it go on me. The whole of mi back wrench out one time ... oh Jesus!

[*He feels a stab of pain.*]

GLORIA: Yuh better let me rub something on it ...

[*JIM waves her off.*]

JIM: The parson, give him him due, never run yet, but when a shot take away him wife handbag, A hear him say, "Let the dead bury the dead, come woman!"

GLORIA: Oh mi God! Poor Pops.

JIM: The timid wife him have there, like she can't mash ants, well she bulldoze three gravestones in her getaway. All dis time A still hang on to Pops. A hang on for dear life. A wasn't running. It was death before humiliation. A hang on till A feel something whistle past mi ears, and A say to miself, "Pops gone already, no further harm can come to him," so A put him down. A couldn't run, even if A did want to. So A lie down beside him and is him save mi life ...

GLORIA: Just like Pops ...

JIM: It wasn't until the police arrive dat things quieten down. A was about six feet from the grave and somehow A manage to get the coffin over to it. When A look in the grave, who yuh think A see down there? Nuh the parson man. One piece o'prayers ... "Oh Lord as yuh raised Lazarus from the dead, deliver me from dis grave." A help to pull him out.

GLORIA: And him help yuh bury him?

JIM: Man never even tell me thanks. The parson run Gloria. Him dat teach me bout faith and prayer, and how to face adversity, him run.

GLORIA: So what about the last rites?

JIM: A bury the old man miself Glo. I say the prayers and I sing the hymn, "Will the circle be unbroken by and by Lord, There's a better home awaits me in the sky Lord, in the sky."

[*Gloria cries.*]

A bury him Glo, and as A walk out of the cemetery I make a decision. The effing gunman and the effing politician not controlling my existence ever again. I talking control of mi life from today. If that could happen to Pops ... A remember the night him took in sick, A took mi life in mi hand and head out into the street. Is nuh little run A run dat night yuh know Gloria ... A run ...

GLORIA: A pray ...

JIM: A dodge ...

GLORIA: Is in my arms him dead. Oh my God, I don't want to remember it.

JIM: A took mi life into mi hands and head out into the street.

GLORIA: A thought you would never make it back.

JIM: Is nuh little run A run dat night, you know, Gloria. A run ...

GLORIA: Him squeeze mi hand and him hold me tight, and him say, "Daughter .... "

JIM: A run ...

GLORIA: A pray ...

JIM: A run, A run, A run. And still A couldn't get through. Them kill Pops! Dis effing country kill Pops. Gloria, believe yuh me when A tell yuh, I want no more part of dis country, and the fuss chance A get to get out, I gone!

GLORIA: Yuh must be hungry.

JIM: A don't want any food, A just want to get out.

GLORIA: Eat first.

JIM: I am full up to here.

[*JIM indicates his neck.*]

GLORIA: Let me get something for miself then ...

JIM: Alright ... bring me a little something.

[*GLORIA goes into the kitchen.*]

Gloria, the children don't know.

GLORIA: They will know somehow.

JIM: Somehow how?

GLORIA: A will ... trust in the Lord. Him will get word to them.

JIM: Is just as well them not here. After that experience A go through today ...

[*Pause... GLORIA speaks as she comes out of the kitchen.*]

GLORIA: It on the fire.

[*There is a pause.*]

JIM: The house quiet, enh?

GLORIA: Not even a gunshot tonight. A can't remember the place so quiet; if it wasn't the children, it was Pops.

JIM: A go miss him yuh know, Gloria ...

GLORIA: Me too.

JIM: A serious, yuh know ....

GLORIA: About what?

JIM: Migrate.

GLORIA: Is not so much that A wanted to go Jim. Is just that A didn't want the children up there by themself.

JIM: Why Pops die? Yuh know? Them tablets never finish just so, y'know. Pops realize that if yuh ever get the chance, yuh would go find the children.

GLORIA: But Jim, him ...

JIM: Is so. Pops clear the way. Is him throw away the tablets.

GLORIA: Don't make me feel like is me kill him ...

JIM: No, Glo. I know yuh did love him, but Pops did what him thought was best.

GLORIA: But dat is suicide, Jim!

JIM: No Glo, sacrifice. We have to go. Pops say so. We can't let him down. So Uncle Sam, we don't know how we coming yet but watch out, coz we coming!

[*BLACKOUT*]

Act I, Scene iii

[*It is late afternoon. JIM is by the refrigerator with a plate in his hands. A small piece of chicken sits in it. He licks his fingers, then returns the plate to the refrigerator. He is heading toward the bedroom when he stops and retraces his steps to the fridge, opens it, takes out the plate, devours the last piece of chicken, and then replaces the plate. He slams the fridge shut and is again heading toward the bedroom when he stops, returns to the fridge, drinks water from the bottle, wipes his hands on a dish cloth which is tied to the refrigerator door, and heads toward the bedroom. At this time, GLORIA, dressed in a duster, is coming on from the bathroom. She is carrying a brown paper bag with a carton of cigarettes in it. The paper bag is tightly wrapped to conceal the cigarettes.*]

JIM: Yuh bring a *Star*?

GLORIA: No. A never see any. Here.

[*She hands JIM a blank passport application form.*]

JIM: Is what?

GLORIA: The passport application form.

[*JIM takes it from her.*]

GLORIA: Yuh take yuh passport picture yet?

JIM: Tomorrow. But we still don't know how we getting up there and A not going up there underground, so we stuck ...

GLORIA: Tell Pops that. What yuh think him would say?

JIM: Yuh right. We have to find a way ...

GLORIA: Whatever the obstacle, Jim. And right now we have to save as much money as we can.

JIM: We can sell the house ....

GLORIA: And if we ever decide to come back?

JIM: Once me step, Gloria, me step.

GLORIA: Even if we was to rent it ...

JIM: Yuh would collect the first month rent and that's it. Sell!

GLORIA: Nobody buying.

JIM: We can't lock it up ... them would capture it before we reach airport.

GLORIA: So what we going do, walk away and leave it? After how we sacrifice to get it? Is not the house so much as the fruit trees. Go water the orange tree for me. Put the hose at the root. It might yet blossom before we have to leave it. A will go look after yuh supper.

[*GLORIA pushes him out. She takes up the package and looks through the window to make sure that he is outside. She then takes a carton of cigarettes from the package and hides it under the dining table. She then goes to the refrigerator. She sees the empty plate.*]

GLORIA: Wretch!

[*She puts the plate in the sink, then returns to the bedroom, collects her makeup kit, returns to the dining room table, and proceeds to do her nails — all the while she is singing a hymn to keep her spirits up. JIM is re-entering.*]

JIM: Gloria, yuh don't start cook yet?

[*She sings louder.*]

Gloria, I am talking to yuh.

GLORIA: No, Jim, A don't start cook yet.

JIM: I hungry bad. What yuh have to eat?

[*He heads into the kitchen.*]

GLORIA: Nutten in there.

[*JIM retraces his steps and heads to the refrigerator.*]

Nutten in there, either.

JIM: Nutten? Not even to make a sandwich?

GLORIA: Nutten.

JIM: Stop paint up yuhself and go cook nuh Gloria ....

GLORIA: Mi nails stay bad enh?

JIM: Gloria, what is dis thing yuh take up of late?

GLORIA: I can't do somet'ing for miself?

JIM: So what happen to me? Leave dat! Go cook!

GLORIA: Not dis evening, Jim. Drink some water and go to yuh bed.

JIM: Gloria, yuh chatting nonsense.

GLORIA: What happen to the leftovers in the fridge?

JIM: Leftovers?

GLORIA: Yes, the chicken wing.

JIM: Oh, A was feeling a little peckish and ...

GLORIA: Dat was yuh supper.

JIM: Gloria, A tired sacrifice!

[*He goes into the bedroom, takes out a shirt, and prepares to go out.*]

GLORIA: Dat chicken was to share for me and yuh.

JIM: Dat little morsel a ...

GLORIA: Yes, and I am without supper coz a you and yuh damn selfishness. One person also can't be expected to sacrifice. Yuh sure that yuh serious about this going to

America?

JIM: How yuh mean!

GLORIA: Well then, get serious. So far A don't see any effort from yuh. All A hear is "Lard Gloria, A hungry.' No more food buying till tomorrow. One night without food won't kill yuh, but it should teach yuh a lesson. Eat off everything one day, yuh do without the next. Yuh have to tighten yuh belt.

[*JIM returns to the dining room. He is almost fully dressed.*]

JIM: The money yuh spen' buying war paint, could buy extra food.

GLORIA: Jim, A have not spent a penny on miself in twenty years.

JIM: And is now yuh starting. Yuh tell me about sacrifice and tighten mi belt. Is sacrifice dis?

[*He picks up her nail polish.*]

GLORIA: Yuh still have money for yuh cigarette though?

JIM: Have which money? For what cigarette?

[*GLORIA takes out a cigarette box.*]

Cigarettes! Where yuh get cigarettes?

GLORIA: No bother long out yuh tongue.

[*JIM reaches for it.*]

Hands off!

JIM: Come nuh, Sister Glo. Free me. From morning A don't smoke a cigarette ...

GLORIA: So why yuh never buy?

JIM: A don't have nuh money. And not one in the shop. They like gold out a street. Where yuh get dat?

GLORIA: Contacts.

JIM: Come nuh ....

GLORIA: Where me and yuh going?

JIM: Don't be unreasonable Gloria. A can do without food, but ease me up with a smoke ...

GLORIA: I buy them to sell.

JIM: Sell me one, then.

GLORIA: A thought yuh never had any money?

JIM: Yuh nuh will credit me.

[*GLORIA laughs.*]

GLORIA: Today A saw a man pay ten cents for a puff. How much puff in a cigarette?

JIM: About ten to fifteen.

GLORIA: One dollar fifty.

[*She is holding out her hand.*]

JIM: Shit! For what?

GLORIA Seeing as is you, give me a dollar.

JIM: Yuh mad ...

GLORIA: Take it or leave it. Is forty dollar A pay for the carton.

JIM: Is a carton yuh have!

[*He goes in search of the carton.*]

GLORIA: And don't bother look for them. A want to make at least sixty dollar profit. A won't satisfy with less.

[*Gloria rests an empty cigarette box on the table.*]

JIM: Yuh is a damn little capitalist.

GLORIA: A praying for the strike prolong, push up the price.

[*JIM is re-entering, sees the pack and inches toward it — he grabs it, triumphant. He opens it. It is empty.*]

JIM: Don't do me them things.

[*GLORIA produces a single cigarette.*]

A will pay yuh later.

GLORIA: No Jim. A know yuh. Put the money on the table.

JIM: A only have eighty cents.

GLORIA: Bring the razor blade ...

[*JIM goes to find a razor blade, then stops.*]

JIM: Yuh going cut it? See the twenty cents ...

GLORIA: On the table.

[*JIM complies. GLORIA gives him the cigarette, then packs up nail polish, etc., and goes into the bedroom. JIM seizes the cigarette with real pleasure and looks around for matches.*]

JIM: Yuh see the matches?

GLORIA: Matches short.

[*JIM continues to look away from GLORIA, who rattles a box. He looks around.*]

JIM: Gimme a light.

GLORIA: Ten cents a stick. Put it on the bed.

JIM: Sister Gloria ...

GLORIA: Don't "Sister Gloria" me. As a matter of fact, get matches where yuh going.

JIM: Where yuh see me going?

GLORIA: G'wan ...

JIM: A just going down the road ...

GLORIA: Yuh going to EAT something.

JIM: How yuh could say a thing like that?

GLORIA: What A say? Notice A don't ask yuh to bring a *piece* for me, coz it wouldn't be to my liking. Today is Tuesday, not even the gunman can keep yuh away from dat little sweetheart.

JIM: Gloria, yuh chatting nonsense. What little sweetheart? A will lock the gate. A soon come ...

GLORIA: Jim, the children not here. Pops gone. Yuh have no reason to lock me in anymore.

JIM: What yuh mean by that?

GLORIA: Take care of yuhself.

JIM: Yuh too ...

GLORIA: I will do just that.

[*She storms into the bedroom, going directly into the bathroom and slamming the door.*]

JIM: Is what do her sah?

[*BLACKOUT*]

Act I, Scene iv

[*JIM comes on from POPS' room. He unlocks the grill gate and continues into the dining area. He gets an idea. He goes to the phone and dials, speaks on phone.*]

JIM: Hey, what's happening? Yuh have anything to eat? ... Eh? ... At home. She gone supermarket ... Hey, listen now, las' night was the greatest y'know ... Honest. The greatest. Is like you make a special effort ... True ... True. The greatest A telling you. Is the greatest plate o' stew peas me ever taste in mi life.

[*GLORIA is heard calling from off.*]

GLORIA: Jim!

[*JIM starts and hurriedly whispers into the phone.*]

JIM: A gone. See you Tuesday.

[*He hangs up.*]

GLORIA: Jim!

JIM: Oi.

GLORIA: Open the door for me....

JIM: Coming ...

[*He unlocks the bolts and GLORIA comes on with two parcels of groceries.*]

Why yuh come home so late?

[*He takes a parcel from her.*]

GLORIA: Is three supermarket A had to go to. One riot to get a little rice.

JIM: Yuh get bread?

[*He bolts the door.*]

GLORIA: Not even a slice.

JIM: Yuh get flour, though?

GLORIA: Get what.

JIM: Serious thing y'know. Is famine on the land.

GLORIA: Yuh can eat out what A get y'see. Is for the week. Jus' rest it on the table.

[*She leaves the dining area with toilet articles, which she takes into the bedroom. At the same time JIM explores the shopping bag, coming up with a roll of toilet paper, then another, then a tin of cleanser — as GLORIA is returning*].

JIM: Gloria.

GLORIA: Enh?

[*JIM notices what she is wearing.*]

JIM: Is mad yuh mad, or is stupid, yuh stupid, or what?

GLORIA: What A do now?

JIM: Is so yuh go to work?

GLORIA: What wrong with me?

JIM: Orange and green. Yuh is a walking target for either side.

GLORIA: A like the combination.

[*She starts to unpack the groceries.*]

JIM: Vanity will be the death of yuh, woman. From now on is brown or blue. Yuh have to dress neutral.

GLORIA: A tired of the madness.

JIM: A school pickney almost meet her death the other day, coz of the color of her uniform. Nobody didn't say anything to yuh on the road?

GLORIA: People was looking on me, yes ...

JIM: So what yuh think? Is admire dem was admiring yuh?

GLORIA: Come. A want to talk to yuh.

[*She heads toward the bedroom and closes the windows.*]

JIM: Is what? .... Don't lock up the house yet....

GLORIA: Shh ... Shh. A don't want nobody know mi business. Read that.

[*She gives him a folded newspaper. He reads from it.*]

JIM: "Want to get to America ..."

[*They look at each other.*]

GLORIA: A went to see him today.

[*She hands JIM a card.*]

Him staying at the Terra Nova.

JIM: Charles E. Wright — Immigration Consultant ... Suite 123, Miami. What color is dis man?

GLORIA: Black, Jamaican, originally from Catadupa, St. James. Him was talking about ackee and saltfish, blue drawers an all dem thing ....

JIM: Could be a trap to get yuh confidence. He could be a C.I.A. agent. Uncle Sam smart. Trust nobody.

GLORIA: We might as well forget it then Jim, coz we can't get up there by weself.

[*She moves away.*]

JIM: Gloria! Gloria, Gloria ... A tell yuh what — A will check him out. Yuh never mention the children?

GLORIA: No.

JIM: Good. What him had to say?

GLORIA: Him suggest a thing name "Identikit."

JIM: What dat?

GLORIA: Him will supply us with a completely new identity. Yuh get it?

JIM: No.

GLORIA: Jim ... Identikit ...

[*He looks blank.*]

We give him we age, an two photograph. Him have a contact in Alabama who will go to a cemetary ...

JIM: Cemetary! Don't mention dat word to me!

GLORIA: Him go to the cemetary an check for a man who born the same year as you. Den him go to the Records Office of Births and Deaths, where him contact have a contact who will destroy the man Death Certificate ....

JIM: Hold on, yuh going too fast ....

GLORIA: Him use your picture, an the dead man birth certificate to apply for a passport ...

JIM: In the dead man name?

GLORIA: It can't be in your name, Jim. Him will do the same for me. Let's say the man name ...

JIM: Mr. Lazarus ...

GLORIA: Yuh t'ink yuh funny, yuh know ....

JIM: If the man come back from the dead, what yuh expect him to name?

GLORIA: Yuh will get a complete record of him life ... from the day him born ...

JIM: Till the day him dead ...

GLORIA: Jim, the man nuh dead....

JIM: A get it now! As far as the world is concerned, the man is still alive....

GLORIA: Yes, Jim, an yuh going to take him place. Yuh passport will show dat yuh arrive in Jamaica for a holiday, so when yuh arrive back in the U.S., yuh just join the returning residents line, and in two twos, yuh gone clear.

JIM: Stop!

GLORIA: What?

JIM: A don't like it.

GLORIA: What wrong with it?

JIM: Let me show yuh what wrong with it. Let's imagine dis is Miami airport. You is Lady Lazarus and yuh arrive from Jamaica, and I is the Immigration Officer standing behind mi desk.

[On these words, JIM moves to stand behind the bed head, using it as a desk.]

GLORIA: Yuh never travel, yet, so what yuh coming with?

JIM: I fix phone at airport. I know how it go.... Come!

[JIM hands her a novel to use as a passport. He sucks at his teeth, begins to chew imaginary gum. He then looks her up and down, and speaks in a psuedo-American accent.]

Git behind the red line, lady.

[GLORIA plays the game. JIM keeps his eyes on the desk in impersonal fashion and stretches out a hand.]

Passport, Madame!

[GLORIA hands it to him. He takes it and, continuing with the imaginary gum chewing, thumbs through it, while looking her up and down. GLORIA has returned to the imaginary red line. JIM continues to look at her suspiciously for a little while. She becomes a little uncomfortable.]

GLORIA: Excuse me, A have to go the bathroom.

[*She is exiting when JIM stops her.*]

JIM: Yuh wretch! Yuh peepee up yuhself right there. A was just waiting to hear yuh accent. As yuh open yuh mouth, the man would buss out a laugh an call the police. A don't like "Identikit." Him don't suggest anything else?

GLORIA: Yeah, but it kinda roundabout.

JIM: It muss be better dan dis Lazarus thing. Let me hear it nuh...

GLORIA: Yuh would have to divorce me.

JIM: No suh! Me not into that. Forget it! After the divorce, what happen?

GLORIA: What a way yuh change yuh mind fast.

JIM: A curious, dat's all.

GLORIA: Den yuh would marry a U.S. citizen. Few months pass, dat divorce come through, yuh legal. A come up, we married again, two o'we legal....

JIM: Then suppose the woman like me?

GLORIA: A know yuh would think o'dat.

JIM: You read me wrong dis time. An even if it was so, A would resist her. What A meant was, what if she like me an want to hold on to me against mi will?

GLORIA: Before yuh married, she would have to sign a paper agreeing to a divorce.

JIM: Ah see what yuh mean. It could work, yes. What yuh say?

GLORIA: No. A know yuh. Bout if she like yuh. How yuh going to resist. Is the last A would see of yuh.

JIM: Gloria, how yuh chat so much nonsense. Look how

long you and me married. Seriously what yuh think?

GLORIA: A have to think 'bout it. Marriage is a sacred thing.

JIM: Yuh rather go to Miami, go peepee up yuhself...

GLORIA: An if the children was to hear ...

JIM: How them to hear. This is a good plan. No risks involved.

GLORIA: On what grounds?

JIM: Time is of the essence. What is the fastest?

GLORIA: Adultery.

JIM: Who commit it?

GLORIA: You!

JIM: Me?!

GLORIA: Up to last Tuesday.

[*JIM laughs.*]

JIM: Gloria ...

GLORIA: What yuh laughing for?

JIM: Yuh make funny joke. A must laugh.

GLORIA: Joke nuh! Yuh think A don't know?

JIM: Gloria, yuh chatting nonsense. A get it! We tell two lie. Say yuh desert the matrimonial home ten years ago. A get two friends swear to it; few weeks later we single again. What yuh say?

GLORIA: It going set we back $2,500 U.S. — Delivered ...

JIM: Blouse beat!

GLORIA: We have to raise it, Jim.

JIM: See the Immigration Consultant. Tell him the deal is on. We will contact him when we ready.

GLORIA: Him leaving Thursday. We will have to contact him in Miami ....

JIM: On the phone? No sah! Letter worse ...

GLORIA: Maybe we could organize a code ....

JIM: Ahm, yes, something like, we got the "H'onions" ...

GLORIA: Nuh bad!

JIM: Touch me....

[*They laugh.*]

Gloria ...

GLORIA: Mmmm ...

JIM: What we would do if dis man was to carry down we life savings?

GLORIA: Hmm, boy Jim, A would have to leave him to God, coz me wouldn't have the heart to pay the $5.00 to kill him.

JIM: If we have $5.00. Hmm ... anyhow ... where we getting the U.S. money?

GLORIA: It on the street.

JIM: Right side the counterfeit?

GLORIA: Is okay. I can get a machine to test the money.

JIM: What kind o' machine?

GLORIA: A little thing, bout dis size. Yuh pass the money over it, and if a red light come on it good.

JIM: Get it. Passing them F.I.U. boys at the airport going call for some real strategy. Gloria, yuh go cook while A put some brain power to dis. Now ...

TWO CAN PLAY

[*GLORIA gets up and is heading to the kitchen.*]

Now where on yuh can A hide dat money?

[*GLORIA stops in surprise.*]

GLORIA: On me? Stop a minute. Is me going up there? A thought it was you, Jim.

JIM: A will go yes, but seeing as how yuh have yuh passport already ...

GLORIA: An yuh don't even take your picture yet ...

JIM: Gloria ...

GLORIA: A tell yuh what, Jim, seeing as how A have to do every thing. Tomorrow A will go and take yuh picture for yuh.

[*She leaves the bedroom and goes to the kitchen.*]

JIM: Dat would be a great help. What yuh say? Yuh think yuh funny, y'know.

[*He follows to bedroom door.*]

[*GLORIA begins to lay the table. She emphasizes her words by plunking down the table mats, plates, knives, forks, etc.*]

GLORIA: More than that ... let me hold mi tongue. No problem, seeing as how A know that when is time to go on the plane, is me going have to go. But dere will be a day of reckoning. The sheep to one side, and the goats to the other.

[*She goes toward bedroom.*]

Let me tell yuh something. A not carrying it in either of those two places....

[*JIM goes off into bathroom and returns with squeezed out toothpaste tube. He tries to get a $2.00 bill into the mouth of the tube. It goes in a little way.*]

JIM: How them say it work? It nuh work. Gimme time. A

must come up with something original to beat them F.I.U. boys.

[*JIM looks around. He sees a Kodak instamatic camera. He looks through it as if to take a picture. He then opens it, takes out the cartridge, and throws the cartridge on the bed.*]

JIM: Hmm, hmm ...

[*He rolls the money, and stuffs it into the camera.*]

This is it! Sister Glo! A get it! A get it! Come quick! This is it!

GLORIA: What happen, why yuh making so much noise?

[*She comes into the bedroom to see JIM with camera in hand, twirling it away.*]

JIM: Ha, check dat.

GLORIA: But, Jim, A can see the money showing through....

JIM: Is so? All yuh have to do is cover it over with yuh hand.

GLORIA: Try again. Is not a bad idea.

[*She goes off into the bathroom. JIM rests the camera on the bedhead and then picks up the toothpaste tube, trying to open the hole as GLORIA shouts from bathroom.*]

How come the toothpaste squeeze out all over the bathroom?

[*She comes out into the bedroom.*]

JIM: I was trying to figure out a way to get the money into the tube.

GLORIA: Then that nuh easy, Jim....

JIM: Do it then, if it so easy.

GLORIA: First thing, yuh shouldn't squeeze out the toothpaste, that not necessary. All yuh have to do is open the bottom, wrap the money in a piece o' plastic, and push it up, and seal it back. Easy as cheese.

JIM: A never realize the bottom could open. How yuh figure it out?

GLORIA: Common sense.

JIM: Yuh see somebody do it. You couldn't figure it out by yuhself.

GLORIA: Why yuh always think A is a damn ass? A figure it out months ago.

JIM: How come, an is jus' dis' evening we start work on it?

GLORIA: How yuh think the children carry money to America? A wasn't sending them on the plane with $56.00 U.S.

JIM: An yuh never say a word to me.

GLORIA: A couldn't say anything to yuh. Yuh too nervous, an them never stop one o' the children.

JIM: A don't trus' you, y'know.

[*He continues to fiddle with the toothpaste tube while GLORIA absentmindedly picks up the camera.*]

GLORIA: Make it rest. Same way the Lord help the children of Israel out of the land of Egypt, him will help us.

[*As she talks she fiddles with the camera.*]

If somehow ...

JIM: What, Glo?

GLORIA: Where the cartridge?

[*JIM points to it on the bed. GLORIA picks it up.*]

Lend me two dollar.

[*JIM gives it to her.*]

Imagine dis is a U.S. $100.00 bill. Lord ...

[*As she says a silent prayer, then tries to put the money into the cartridge.*]

It going in, Jim! It going in!

JIM: It going in, Glo!

GLORIA: It gone in, Jim.

[*JIM takes the cartridge and camera from her and puts cartridge in camera.*]

JIM: What A tell yuh 'bout me, man.

[*Then he sings*]

Onward Christian Soldiers ...

[*He puts the camera to his eyes, focusing on GLORIA as he continues singing.*]

JIM: Click!!

[*BLACKOUT*]

Act I, Scene v

[*"Onward Christian Soldiers" continues over till the lights come up again. GLORIA enters from the bathroom, goes to the dining area, and looks through the peepholes at the side of the front door. There is no one there — she fidgets, checks the time, takes water from the refrigerator but does not drink. She returns to the window, looks again and sees JIM. She unbolts the front door. JIM comes on immediately.*]

GLORIA: Yuh get it?

JIM: Yes.

GLORIA: Yuh tes' it?

JIM: No. Not yet.

GLORIA: Jesus Christ, Jim!

JIM: It wasn't convenient.

GLORIA: How yuh mean?

JIM: Is a dread place A had to go to. A couldn't tes' it in front of the men.

GLORIA: Why not? Is money we dealing with.

JIM: The men touchy y'know. Them don't know me. Yuh don't understand. Is a contact of a contact. Next thing A bring out the tester to test the money, they think A is undercover police and shoot me. To tell you the truth, A never thought A would leave there alive. Suppose me contact set me up — A had an uneasy feeling that somebody was following me. One round d' round A had to take to come home.

GLORIA: Yuh really go buy puss in a bag Jim. Dey would have to kill me. What now if is counterfeit yuh get?

JIM: Don't say so ... test it and make me know mi fate.

GLORIA: Is me must test it? No sir! If we get carry down, we get carry down already.

JIM: Don't talk so loud. A say A would test it after A leave the place, but A couldn't very well tes' it on the bus.

[*JIM goes into his shoes, takes money out, gives it to her.*]

GLORIA: Lawd, dis husband o' mine. If nuh for his sake, den for mine, make dem good. So lock the window

[*He is in the process of doing so, when there is a knock.*]

Is who dat?

JIM: A don't expect anybody. Hide the money!

[*She hides it under a pillow — then sits on it. He leaves the bedroom very tentatively and goes into the dining area. He looks through the peepholes at front door. He panics. He bobs and weaves back into the bedroom.*]

JIM: Jesus Christ, Gloria!!

GLORIA: Is what!!!

JIM: Dem set me up!

GLORIA: Is what!!!

JIM: Police!

GLORIA: Police??!!

[*JIM and GLORIA are in a state of high panic. JIM is completely confused.*]

JIM: A whole battalion. Rass! Bring the money. Go through the back. Bury it in the back yard.

[*GLORIA is on her way there, when she sees the policemen in the back yard.*]

GLORIA: Dem round the back too, Jim. Dem surround the yard.

JIM: A will go out to dem, you go in the bathroom. Flush it!

GLORIA: But Jim ...

JIM: Do what A tell yuh, Gloria. Flush it! Anyplace we hide it, dem will find it, so flush it!

GLORIA: But Jim ...

JIM: Is jail dat ...

[*Knock, knock ... "Police" ... from offstage.*]

JIM: Coming ...!!

[*GLORIA disappears into the bathroom. A police siren is heard. JIM exits to the outside ... GLORIA comes on and walks tentatively to the grill gate. Jim is entering.*]

JIM: Gloria. Gloria — yuh did what A tell yuh?

GLORIA: Yes.

JIM: Jesus God!

GLORIA: What happen?

JIM: Yuh flush it?

GLORIA: Yes Jim.

JIM: Everything gone to rass!!

GLORIA: What happen? Where the police?

JIM: Them gone.

GLORIA: Say what?!

JIM: Wrong house. They had a report about a prowler at No. 13. They got the numbers mixed up an come to 30 instead. Yuh flush it Gloria?

GLORIA: Yes Jim.

[*JIM is crying like a baby.*]

JIM: Yuh certain yuh flush it?

[*She nods.*]

GLORIA: All gone. I know how yuh feel, but is alright. Look at it dis way. It might have been counterfeit.

JIM: Mi whole life, Gloria.

GLORIA: On the other hand, it might have been good money.... The value of the property gone up, dats all. Anytime yuh sit on the seat now, yuh will be sitting on a gold mine.

JIM: Is nuh time fer joke.

GLORIA: What yuh want me to do? Bawl? If A start to bawl, A won't stop.

JIM: After all the starvation; is better A did eat it.

GLORIA: It would gone down the drain same way.

JIM: We divorce for nutten Gloria. All to naught.

GLORIA: Look on the bright side, Jim. F.I.U. might have catch me at the airport...

JIM: You right ... A going kill meself ... A dead as it is .... yuh have a piece of rope?

GLORIA: Jim, is alright, nuh fret yuhself ... A never flush it ....

JIM: The way things is, A can't even afford to kill miself....

GLORIA: Jim, A say A never flush it ...

JIM: Say what! But how come yuh tell me ...

GLORIA: Let dis be a lesson to yuh. For a man who say him is the General, you too quick to panic.

[*She goes into the bathroom and returns with the money still wrapped in its plastic. It is dripping wet, but secure.*]

JIM: After all the trouble, A only hope now say them good.

GLORIA: Is dat now — tester?

JIM: Tester! Oh!

[*He goes to where he had hidden it. He gives it to GLORIA.*]

GLORIA: Say yuh prayers.

[*JIM prays as she unwraps money and runs a note over the tester.*]

JIM: Red light!

GLORIA: Thank yuh Jesus!

JIM: Solid!

[*She tests another note.*]

GLORIA: Thank yuh Lord.

JIM: Solid Gold!

[*She tests another one.*]

GLORIA: Amen!

JIM: Is time to call Miami.... We got the Onions.

[*He does a little dance.*]

[*GLORIA starts to sing.*]

GLORIA: At the Cross, at the Cross ...

[*She continues to test the money. JIM picks up the phone.*]

JIM: Operator? Get me Miami 305-6l2-6211 ... Charles E. Wright ... James Thomas ... I'll hold.

[*GLORIA leaves the bedroom and goes toward JIM by the phone, her eyes filled with tears.*]

GLORIA: Jim everything solid....

[*JIM extends his arm to her and encircles her with it.*]

TREVOR RHONE

JIM: Oh Gloria! We ready! Dis is it! Start to pack! Book yuh ticket. Uncle Sam, we is on yuh door step. We gone clear.

[*JIM is talking on the telephone.*]

Hello!

[*The lights fade on them.*]

Act II, Scene i

[*JIM enters from the bathroom, carrying a radio. It is playing hard acid rock. He stops, switches stations. He tunes in to a Miami station.*]

ANNOUNCER:

This is WINZ, Miami — under cloudy skies with a 40 percent chance of rain. It's 7:45 in the swinging city, and right now let's swing along with Glenn Miller and his orchestra "In the Mood."

[*As JIM leaves the bedroom and goes toward the dining area, he dances to the music. Then a helicopter is heard overhead. It drowns out the radio.... He goes to the window, as the helicopter lights are seen.*]

JIM: Shine yuh lights, Soldier Boy. Shine yuh light. Circle and come back. Don't forget, alright.

[*As he waves to the departing copter, he turns off the radio. It is quiet, he is restless. His eyes light on the photographs of his children.*]

JIM: Boy Paul, you alright? You see yuh mother up there? No? Three weeks now she leave, not a word from her. Anyway, you take care till A come up; and take care of Andrew...Tell him to work hard at school.

[*He moves to Suzie's picture*]

An Suzie girl, A will make it up to yuh. We going be a family again.

[*He looks in the direction of Pops' room and talks at the door.*]

You going be there too, enh Pops ... Answer me then, nuh. A know yuh in the house. A hear yuh last night. Ha, ha ... Alright, time to take a five.

[He takes GLORIA's picture down, and goes to the bedroom, which is very untidy, as is the rest of the house. He talks directly to the photograph.]

JIM: Sister Glo, yuh okay? A don't know why A can't get it out o' mi head dat something wrong.

[He puts the photograph down on the dressing table, then tries to make the bed. He finds a pack of biscuits among the sheets. He dusts the ants away.]

JIM: Damn ants, want bite me on mi willie nuh...

[He eats a biscuit, then returns to the photograph. He looks at it while he sits on the bed.]

JIM: You still look okay. What happening to me? After 20 years ... Dis is madness....

[He pauses.]

Another Tuesday night. No.

[Another pause.]

Hmmmm ... Mi hair drop out already as it is ... Why yuh watching me so?

[He turns her picture around. He turns the radio on and puts out the light. Music is loud and orgasmic for 10 to 15 seconds. JIM is in bed masturbating. Then the lights are switched on ... JIM panics.]

JIM: Lord ha'mercy.

[He comes up from under the sheets to see GLORIA. She lowers the volume on the radio.]

GLORIA: A need 25 dollars for the taxi....

JIM: Ahm, look in mi trousers....

GLORIA: Where is it?

JIM: Ahm, over dey.

GLORIA: A don't see it.

JIM: It over dey man.

GLORIA: Jesus Christ, Jim, the taxi waiting. Get up nuh.

[*As she tries to pull the covers off him, he hangs on tight.*]

JIM: Look on the bureau.

[*GLORIA finds the money and goes out. JIM jumps to a sitting position, checks that GLORIA has gone out, then wraps the sheet around himself, gets up, checks bed for any telltale signs, and then goes to the bathroom. The stage is empty for a beat. GLORIA comes on in the living room, puts her suitcase down, surveys the mess.*]

GLORIA: Jim ...

[*She enters the bedroom, notices her picture turned around. He enters, sheet wrapped around him.*]

JIM: Yuh come.

GLORIA: Dats all yuh have to say to me —"Yuh come"? A come home and is so yuh greet me. Yuh couldn't even get out o' the damn bed ...

JIM: A was feeling chilly ...

GLORIA: Chilly! Three weeks A was freezing mi ass off up dere, an yuh tellin' me yuh was chilly.

JIM: A glad yuh come.

GLORIA: A see the proof.

JIM: What yuh say?

GLORIA: What happen? Yuh thought A was dead?

JIM: It cross mi mind, yes. A never see yuh come back, and A didn't know what happen to yuh ...

GLORIA: So dat's why yuh turn mi picture around?

JIM: Picture? What? Oh dat. A was dusting, y'know, cobwebbing. Oh yes, A remember now. A turn the picture to cobweb it, when A heard a knocking at the gate. A forget to turn it back ...

[*He reverses it.*]

GLORIA: So yuh was cobwebbing?!

JIM: Yeah, man ... so tell me.

GLORIA: A must say yuh did a nice job. The house really sparkling.

[*She goes into the bathroom.*]

JIM: Pshaw! Don't deal with me so.

GLORIA: Jim, man! Come here!

JIM: A know, A know. In dere stay bad.

[*GLORIA is returning to the bedroom.*]

GLORIA: Yuh don't do one thing in the house since A gone.

JIM: Feget bout the house nuh and tell me, how yuh do?

GLORIA: A'm okay. How you do?

JIM: A'm okay. How it went? Yuh married?

[*She shows him the ring.*]

Ha, ha, ha! An yuh legal?

GLORIA: All the way.

JIM: Yuh really legal?

GLORIA: Yes, Jim!

JIM: Yuh hear dat, Pops. She legal! Gloria, legal ...

[*He dances around ... he is high as a kite. She is very low keyed.*]

What happen? Yuh don't look happy.

GLORIA: We will talk.

JIM: What happen?

GLORIA: A will talk to yuh.

[*She leaves toward the dining area.*]

JIM: Something wrong. Yuh suppose to be jumping for joy. Is what?

GLORIA: Is just dat ... Well ... First of all, dem search me at the airport, y'know.

JIM: Say what!?

GLORIA: Strip me stark born naked.

JIM: Jesus Christ, yuh lie....

GLORIA: Honest to God. A say, when the man take up the film, A tell him mi sister was here on holiday and forget dem, den him toss dem one side ...

JIM: Wheww!!

GLORIA: Den him ask me, "Whey the onions?"

JIM: To rass! How dem know?

GLORIA: Who yuh talk to?

JIM: A never talk to nobody.

GLORIA: Yuh sure?

JIM: Positive.

GLORIA: So it got to be on the phone.

JIM: From the night A go buy the money, A had an uneasy feeling that dem had me under wraps. So what yuh say?

GLORIA: A bluff him. A say "What onions? So much onions in Miami, what A carrying onion up there for?" Him look on me an say "Go on."

[*JIM hisses.*]

JIM: Damn little F.I.U. bwoy dem; think dem can match wits wid me! Dem is amateur! What A tell yuh, Gloria, I is the General. Dem could search till thy kingdom come, dem would never find where I put dat money....

GLORIA: Whey *YOU* put it!?! Nuh me come up with the idea? An stop dat nonsense bout yuh is the General, General mi ass!

JIM: Why yuh getting so hot under the collar?

GLORIA: I take all the risk!

JIM: Okay, okay, yuh good too ...

GLORIA: Good too!! Why it so hard for yuh to admit dat A worth something?!

JIM: A was running a little joke ...

GLORIA: Joke?!! A know yuh!! Now A go an come back yuh can say anything ... bout yuh is the General. So is you mastermind it for them to search me at the airport, an make me miss mi plane?

JIM: Yuh miss the plane?

GLORIA: So when A reach Miami, the man wasn't dere to meet me.

JIM: So what yuh do, Gloria?

GLORIA: A phone him number 'bout ten times. No answer.

JIM: Jesus!

GLORIA: A took stock o' mi situation. A had to find a place to sleep. Dem had a hotel in the airport, but when dem tell me the price, A say no.

JIM: How much so?

GLORIA: Sixty dollars U.S., plus tax.

JIM: For the week ...

GLORIA: For the night!

JIM: At the rate A buy the money?!! Blouse beat! So what yuh do Gloria?

GLORIA: A decide to sit it out at the airport. Den a next panic lick me. Is Friday A go up. Suppose the man don't work again till Monday?

JIM: Him work on Saturday, Gloria?

GLORIA: Wait nuh, Jim.

JIM: Don't keep me in suspense, man....

[*GLORIA begins to re-enact the events in Miami.*]

GLORIA: A take up a seat, lap mi foot over the suitcase, and clutch mi handbag. A watch the time. A get up and A walk; A walk; A tired; A doze off; A wake up.

JIM: Him work Saturday, Gloria?

GLORIA: A wake up an see two suspicious looking white bwoy eyeing me. A clutch mi handbag.

JIM: Cuban dem nuh!

GLORIA: A wouldn't know if dem was Cuban, Jim; but A couldn't sleep out there. A had to go bathroom an it come to me dat in there would be the safest place to sleep.

[*JIM turns up his nose.*]

So A nap, and suddenly A wake up, and when A look under the door, A see a shoes. Something never right bout dem shoes. Den it hit me! It was a man shoes.

JIM: Is in the man toilet yuh go sleep, Gloria?

GLORIA: A draw up miself in a little ball, tight, tight ...

[*She enacts it.*]

And A pray. The shoes don't move. Den A see when him hand come down, den piece o' him head.

JIM: Him checking if yuh in dey!

GLORIA: A tighten up miself even more. Him couldn't see me. Few seconds later, him walk 'way. A listen for the door, den A fly out.... Outside A see one o' the white bwoy dat was eyeing mi handbag, and when A look on him shoes ...

JIM: The same Cuban bwoy ...

GLORIA: The same shoes ...

JIM: Is Cuban definitely. Yuh can always tell a Cuban by him shoes.

GLORIA: A walk up and down all night.

JIM: Him work Saturday, Gloria?

GLORIA: Yes. Him work Saturday.

JIM: Problem solved!

GLORIA: Dats what you think. A had to find mi way up dey. Him give me one set o' directions — north, west, den go east on l77, an all dem kinda thing. A couldn't make head nor tail o' the directions.

JIM: Is so Uncle Sam scientific — none o' dis turn right, turn left business.

GLORIA: Well, is the turn right, turn left business A accustomed to. So by the time A reach outside the airport is lost A lost.

JIM: Den yuh nuh catch yuh directions off the sun, Baby. It rise in the west, set in the east; north, south.

GLORIA: It rise in the *east* Jim....

JIM: Is so? You have to be nautical....

GLORIA: Yuh can chat. Yuh wasn't up dey. A porter carry mi little suitcase couple feet, an when him put it down him say, "You won't see me again." So A tell him "Ba Bye." The man say ...

[*She speaks louder.*]

"You won't see me again" ... so A look on him, an he shove him hand under mi nose an say "You can tip me now!" So A give him a dollar.

JIM: Is the system, Gloria. Uncle Sam organize it dat everybody can make a buck.

GLORIA: A had to take two bus....

JIM: Yuh ride on the luxury bus, Gloria? Dem nice, enh!

GLORIA: Not the one I ride on to Liberty City. A sit down on the tough seat an watch the fancy tall building with the white people get lower an lower, till dem reach shack with black people, an A was in the heart of the ghetto.

JIM: Gloria, yuh sure is America yuh go?

GLORIA: Yes Jim. A was up dey. An A come off the bus, an had to walk 'mongst the pushers, the winos, an the addicts. All eyes on me! A nuh little guard. A guard mi handbag ...

JIM: If dat damn Jamaican from Catadupa did pick yuh at the airport, all dat wouldn't happen to yuh.

GLORIA: A glad him never come Jim. A learn 'bout the place. A don't think A would ever forget. A stop at a furniture factory to ask directions, an as A approach, a white man say, "What yuh want?" so A show him the piece of paper with the address, an him say, "We don't give directions —GET LOST!" An A hear him say to him friend, "Nigger ..."

JIM: What!!! Who him talking to? Who him calling Nigger? So what yuh do? Yuh didn't kick him in him ... Yuh have him address? Yuh wait till A get up there.

GLORIA: The eye water roll down mi face, as A head back out in the rain an stop a taxi.

JIM: Is the South — we don't have to go there....

GLORIA: The taxi man drive me round an round, an after 'bout ten minutes him let me off in front o' the building, which was right round the corner from the furniture factory.

JIM: Damn tief. Dat happen all over the world all the same....

GLORIA: A walk up the stairs to the consultant place, an A say to miself "Lord whey A going?" Yuh see the fancy card the man give me, Suite 1-2-3? Is a little dutty place wid one typewriter an a fish tank wid a dead fish. Him take me to some dingy little apartment, an tell me the wedding was in a few days time. A jam someting behind the door an try to sleep. I hear gun shot same way.

JIM: Up dey?

GLORIA: An siren keeping me awake all night.

[*Shots*]

JIM: Lock up the house.

[*JIM secures the bolts, etc. in living room. GLORIA lifts suitcase into the bedroom. Then he follows her.*]

GLORIA: I am home! Boy, Jim, A am having some serious reservation 'bout this America thing, y'know.

JIM: Say what? Reser .... what? Gloria, A don't say yuh didn't have one or two bad experience, but as A say ...

GLORIA: Jim, even the man A married think A would be an ass to leave what A have here, an him is a native. Him take me round an show me....

JIM: Wait a minute, Gloria. Yuh an dis man chat? A think

TWO CAN PLAY

yuh jus' see him, marry him, an leave him. How come him taking yuh 'round?

GLORIA: We had to live together Jim .... Jim. Jim — don't jump to conclusions, let me tell yuh how it went. It was the consultant who insist we stay together. Dere's dis interview before yuh get yuh residency papers, an we had to be prepared for it. Is to make sure yuh don't get married just to get the U.S. visa, like the Immigration man suggest I do. A had to look him straight in the eye an say, "Sir, I got married for love." I was in one room, an mi husband in the other, an is one intimate question after another ... like what color nighties A wear to bed last night. At the same time dem cross check an ask the man the same question.

JIM: Him sleep dey Gloria?

GLORIA: Yes Jim. On the couch.

JIM: Him try anything Gloria?

GLORIA: No Jim....

JIM: Him rape yuh Gloria?

GLORIA: A say No Jim.

JIM: Him never had to rape yuh. All him had to do was demand him legal rights. Him rape yuh Gloria?

GLORIA: No Jim.

JIM: Yuh fight him off ...

GLORIA: Dere was no need to. Him never try anything.

JIM: Yuh can't scream. Yuh can't call Police. What yuh do Gloria?

GLORIA: Jim. A say the man never try anything.

JIM: Him never even ask for a little cheups?

[*Makes the sound of a kiss.*]

TREVOR RHONE

GLORIA: No.

JIM: Is a miracle! The man yuh married is either a angel, a battyman or a cripple.

GLORIA: I wouldn't know, Jim.

JIM: Is what kinda man dis man?

GLORIA: Who, Johnny?

JIM: Johnny? Johnny what him name?

GLORIA: Johnny Peters the Third.

JIM: So yuh is ...

GLORIA: For the time being, Jim.

JIM: What him look like?

GLORIA: Black, fortyish, sorta resemble Pops in him younger days.

JIM: Pops was a good-looking man. What him do up dey?

GLORIA: Him is a animal control officer.

JIM: Say what?

GLORIA: A dog catcher, Jim....

JIM: Gloria, yuh serious?

GLORIA: Nutten wrong wid it. Job is job....

JIM: Him would do well down here.... Him could catch flea for all A care. Him serve him purpose. Thank yuh Lord. It is all over. When A think o' what we go through. Is a high price we pay for dat visa.

GLORIA: A don't think it worth the price, Jim. Is two America. White America, Black America. Which one yuh going to? A check out a lot o' things up dere — job, housing. At least we don't owe nutten on dis.

JIM: Gloria, we gone too far. We can't turn back now. A have a man coming to buy the house. Gloria, yuh feget we not doing dis for weself.... Pops sacrifice him life so dat we could be wid the children....

GLORIA: Jim, maybe we read him wrong....

JIM: Gloria, yuh chatting nonsense....

GLORIA: Don't tell me dat again, Jim!

[*She shouts at him.*]

JIM: What come over yuh woman?

GLORIA: A'm telling yuh how A feel, an what A think, an yuh call it nonsense. Maybe what Pops was saying is, dat is time yuh stop treating me like shit!

JIM: Gloria!!!

GLORIA: A tell yuh what Jim. Is minimum six months before we can go up dey, so we have time to think 'bout it.

JIM: Gloria ...

GLORIA: Make it rest for now....

JIM: Cool....

GLORIA: Okay.

[*JIM makes another attempt to discuss the matter.*]

Jim!!

JIM: I did all buy a bottle o' Wincarnis to celebrate. I might as well drink it.

[*He is going toward the dining area.*]

GLORIA: Pour me a little.

[*JIM is amazed that GLORIA has made a demand of him. He stops and returns to the bedroom to reassert his position of authority.*]

JIM: All the glasses dutty. Go wash two, an while yuh in the kitchen, fix me something nice to eat, A sorta peckish. A haven't had a decent meal since yuh leave.

GLORIA: Yuh little people never feed yuh!

JIM: Yuh come back wid dat nonsense Gloria. Look how mi hand burn up.

[*She looks at it.*]

A was trying to light the stove.

[*She looks at him blankly*].

Yuh shoulda seen it the first day.

GLORIA: Yuh poor thing....

JIM: It almost burn down the house.

GLORIA: Hmm ...

JIM: Bread outside. Just rustle up something nice to put in between it....

GLORIA: Not tonight, Jim....

JIM: Come nuh, sweetness....

[*He gets physical in an attempt to sweeten her up.*]

GLORIA: Nuh bother.

[*She pushes him off.*]

JIM: Come nuh, man. A really hungry, yuh know. A will go try light the stove....

[*He goes out.*]

GLORIA: If yuh think I going into dat dutty kitchen tonight, yuh have anodder guess coming!!

[*JIM stops in the dining room when he realizes that GLORIA is not following him.*]

TWO CAN PLAY

JIM: Gloria!

GLORIA: Yes, Jim.

JIM: Come here.

GLORIA: If yuh want me, come to me....

JIM: No man! Yuh come!

[*He tries to reassert his dominance.*]

GLORIA: Stay out there then.

[*JIM returns to the bedroom area and sees her in a state of half undress.*]

JIM: Gloria, what game yuh playing wid me tonight? Come here to me an stop yuh nonsense....

[*He tries a little sexual blackmail.*]

GLORIA: No, Jim. No!

[*He continues his assault.*]

A will scream!

JIM: Scream then.

[*She screams.*]

Yuh mad woman!!!

GLORIA: Take what A say serious, Jim. When A say "No," A mean no....

JIM: What happen to yuh?

GLORIA: Right now, we not married, y'know....

JIM: So?

GLORIA: So don't take anyting for granted. Look now. If yuh serious 'bout going to America, we going have to remarry, but before we do dat, yuh going have to court me again.

TREVOR RHONE

JIM: But is what yuh come back wid. What yuh say? Court yuh? Court yuh how?

GLORIA: *You* know. Yuh did it before...

[*JIM falls on his knees.*]

JIM: Oh Gloria, Victoria, h'apple of my h'eye, love of mi life ...

GLORIA: What yuh say yuh doing?

JIM: Yuh say A must court yuh.

GLORIA: A serious, yuh know. A'm not going back into it under the same conditions. Dere's going have to be a new understanding. All dem things like "Feed me" ... whether A sick, A dying, or just come off the plane, "Feed me" ....

JIM: A think yuh woulda been happy to do something for me, after all is three weeks ...

GLORIA: Jim, is twenty years o' "Feed me." "Feed me" is done!

JIM: Feed me dis one last time....

GLORIA: Yuh think A joking.

[*Pause*]

JIM: Alright den. Come we go to bed.

GLORIA: Yuh think *dat* will make me change mi mind. Y'know what, A going sleep in Pop's room ....

JIM: Gloria ...

GLORIA: From now on regard me as a guest, an A expect yuh to treat yuh guest accordingly. If yuh really serious bout marrying me again, yuh can start by cleaning up the house, an washing up the dutty dishes. See yuh in the morning. An A plan to lock the door.

[*She goes.*]

JIM: What the ASS. Mi marriage wash up over a sandwich?

[*BLACKOUT*]

Act II, Scene ii

[*It is the following day. The lights come up on JIM making the bed, fluffing out the pillows and doing it very well. He picks up GLORIA's shoes, mutters under his breath about having to do woman's work. He leaves the bedroom, taking the radio with him, and puts it on the shelf in the dining area. The dining table is a mess of dirty plates, etc. JIM looks at them maliciously, then he collects them and exits to the kitchen offstage. A few moments pass, then the sound of plates breaking. Soon after, JIM returns to the dining area with four plates. He is about to smash another when he hears GLORIA coming.*]

JIM: Bitch!

[*He puts the plates away quickly as GLORIA enters through the front door.*]

GLORIA: What's happening?

JIM: I am here

[*GLORIA goes into the kitchen. JIM watches her. He waits for her outburst over the broken plates. GLORIA returns, says nothing, and is going to the bedroom.*]

JIM: Yuh have a *Star*?

[*She gives it to him and continues toward the bedroom. JIM watches her, uncertain; then he follows her.*]

Alright! Cuss me. Get it over with.

GLORIA: Cuss yuh? What for?

JIM: 'Bout the plates.

GLORIA: A muss cus' yuh, Jim?

JIM: Is some o' yuh best crockery. I know dat.

GLORIA: Them was yuh wedding present as much as mine. How much yuh bruck?

JIM: Yuh mean how much drop out o' mi hand an bruck.... Six ...

GLORIA: Is okay. A wouldn't worry bout it.

JIM: A thought yuh woulda been mad.

[*He returns to the dining table.*]

GLORIA: No. Practice make perfect. If yuh have to bruck all o' dem, so be it. Yuh have to learn....

[*Pause*]

JIM: So Gloria ...

GLORIA: Yes, Jim ...

JIM: What yuh doing out on the street till now?

GLORIA: A guess A better warn yuh. A'm starting evening classes at St. John's College ... three evenings a week.

JIM: When yuh decide dat?

GLORIA: Is something A always wanted to do.

JIM: Yuh could at least have discussed it with me.

GLORIA: A did — years ago....

JIM: Say what?

GLORIA: Guess yuh don't remember what yuh say to me ...

JIM: No. Remind me.

GLORIA: "So who will look after the children?" Well the children not here, and Pops gone, so —classes run 5:30 to 7:30.

JIM: What kinda classes?

GLORIA: I am planning to be a nurse....

JIM: At your age? I hear bout Florence Nightingale, but what yuh planning to be — Florence Fowl?

[*GLORIA looks at him, then goes to the dining area.*]

So who will look after mi food when I come home hungry at night?

GLORIA: Yuh will have to learn to fend for yuhself in the kitchen; so yuh better come watch what A doin'....

JIM: A don't understand yuh. Yuh leave here a perfectly normal good woman, yuh go to America for three weeks, and yuh come back with all dem corrupt new-fangle ideas. Who influence yuh?

GLORIA: A have a mind of mi own. Why yuh think somebody have to influence me?

JIM: But must. Is not so yuh leave here.

GLORIA: Same person go, same person come.

JIM: No sir!

GLORIA: A just never confident myself to talk to yuh before, an insist dat yuh listen to me.

JIM: Gloria, A don't understand what's going on. First yuh want me to wash plate, now yuh want me to cook, an dis thing 'bout going to school! What happen, we not going to 'Merica?

GLORIA: I not qualified for anything, yuh know. An if A go to America — IF — we don't decide yet — A not going up there to clean white people floor. So A determined to go to school. But right now I need yuh help....

JIM: Why all the changes?

GLORIA: A not asking for much....

[*JIM hisses his teeth.*]

GLORIA: Why yuh have to be so discouraging? For once in yuh life, help me to do something for ME nuh man.... Come nuh man ... A will show yuh what to do.

[*There is a long pause as JIM ponders his decision.*]

JIM: What yuh cooking?

GLORIA: Mince. Yuh can wash the rice.

JIM: Pass the soap.

GLORIA: To do what?

JIM: Wash the rice.

GLORIA: Sometimes A wonder if yuh really have sense. Catch some water. I will show yuh.

[*JIM goes off to get the water, as she gets the rice. He returns.*]

JIM: Uncle Ben's. Yuh bring dis back with yuh?

GLORIA: Yes. Measure it out. One cup to two cups water.

JIM: Dis is the real thing. The Rolls Royce of Rice. Genuine American. This can eat by itself.

[*They measure.*]

Is years A don't do this.

GLORIA: Yuh use to cook?

JIM: When A was a little boy go to spend time in the country, A use to cook in the bush.

GLORIA: So how come yuh can't cook rice?

[*Goes off with rice to kitchen.*]

JIM: Rice was a luxury in dem days. Is banana, breadfruit, yampi A use to deal with. Cook up with salt pork in a kerosene pan ... den yuh eat it out banana leaf. Sweet!

GLORIA: Yuh have to give me the recipe.

JIM: How much salt?

GLORIA: Do yuh thing, man.

[*He finds the salt, sprinkles the food, then throws some over his shoulders.*]

JIM: Cool. Where the *Onions*.

[*They laugh at this reference. She gets it from the refrigerator and gives it to him.*]

Is Uncle Sam feeding us.

GLORIA: Is our fault dat.

JIM: Black pepper.

[*He sprinkles generously.*]

Is not bad fun....

GLORIA: Is the first time we ever do anything together.

JIM: Dat not true, Gloria.

GLORIA: Apart from *dat*....

JIM: No. Yuh remember when we was courting?

[*He laughs.*]

All the times A took yuh to play cricket with the boys?

GLORIA: It was my job to field.

[*JIM stops cooking and picks up an object which he uses as a bat and goes through the motion of playing strokes.*]

JIM: An yuh wasn't a bad fielder, for a woman ...

GLORIA: A never get a chance to bat, though....

JIM: How yuh mean? Woman can't bat!

GLORIA: Yuh never try me.

JIM: Yuh really wanted to bat?

GLORIA: Yes.

JIM: Why yuh didn't say so?

GLORIA: And what yuh would say — "GLORIA, GO FIELD!"

JIM: An after the game, we would go traipsing through Race Course hand in hand, an yuh would look on me with yuh goat eye....

GLORIA: Mi one regret, 'bout dem days, is we never sit down an chat.

JIM: Say we never chat....

GLORIA: We chat yes, but we never discuss what we wanted out of life; what we wanted out of the marriage. We never really get to know each other, Jim....

JIM: The only way we never get to know each other was in the Biblical way. Nuh true? All the time the Parson was saying the vows, is one thing was on mi mind.

[*He tries to caress her.*]

GLORIA: A know dat. Behave yuhself, Jim.

JIM: Exact same thing yuh use to say. "Behave yuhself, Jim."

[*He touches her again.*]

GLORIA: Don't do dat....

JIM: Yuh hold out on me bad, y'know. Oh boy. A will never forget the first time. What a night dat was. You remember it, Gloria?

[*JIM's face is alive with pleasurable memories, while GLORIA's reflects her bad times.*]

Oh boy. Hmmm, it was worth waiting for. Still is. But

Gloria, all the times yuh tell me no, yuh didn't want to do it too?

GLORIA: What yuh think?

JIM: Dat no. A know yuh as a woman of principle. Nuh so?

GLORIA: No.

JIM: How yuh mean no. Yuh wanted to do it before we married?

GLORIA: Wanted to do it, yes.

JIM: 'Onest!?

GLORIA: It was a serious thing....

JIM: Is so? So what yuh do? Take a cold shower?

GLORIA: Well ...

[*She laughs.*]

What yuh do, Jim?

JIM: Go for a ride on mi bicycle. What yuh do?

GLORIA: Why yuh want to know?

JIM: A just curious.

GLORIA: A will tell yuh....

JIM: Now, man....

GLORIA: A soon come.

[*She goes into the kitchen.*]

JIM: Gloria, come here....

GLORIA: What?

JIM: What yuh use to do?

GLORIA: A will whisper an tell yuh....

JIM: Why yuh can't say it out loud?

GLORIA: A just ...

JIM: Alright! Whisper!

[*She goes up to him and whispers.*]

A didn't hear yuh. Come again.

[*She whispers in his ear for the second time.*]

Gloria, yuh really do dat?

GLORIA: A know A shouldn't tell yuh....

JIM: Woman don't do dem things....

GLORIA: Yuh do it, though....

JIM: Me? Yuh must be crazy. Yuh think I want hair grow in mi hand middle?

[*He looks at his palm — then double takes.*]

It nuh right.... A guess if it was before we married. But since den yuh been getting the real thing, enh? Enh Gloria?

GLORIA: Aye, Jim....

JIM: What yuh mean by dat? Yuh do it since, Gloria? A ask yuh a question. Yuh do it since we married?

GLORIA: Yes, Jim?!

JIM: Yes yuh answer me, or yes yuh do it?

GLORIA: Yes. A do it!

[*There is a long pause. JIM is stunned. He looks away, then directly at her. Then looks off again. Hisses. There is a silence. She goes to the bathroom.*]

JIM: The woman leave the bridal suite, leave me, to go do dat!

[*His eyes light on a tin of Baygon spray. He picks it up and*

TWO CAN PLAY

goes after her.]

Gloria, show me mi competition. Show me!!

GLORIA: Why yuh behaving so? At leas' A never go outside an look for a man.

JIM: Is better if yuh do dat. What yuh do nuh natural. What yuh use?

GLORIA: Jim, stop questioning me....

JIM: Yuh tell me say yuh do it. Yuh might as well tell me what yuh use.

GLORIA: It was in the bathroom, Jim.

JIM: With what?

GLORIA: With the water.

JIM: The water? Them things I read bout in dutty book, you introduce into mi yard? Jesus Christ. Is nuh one or two times the Water Commission come check the meter. Nutten wrong with it. Now I know!

GLORIA: Why yuh behaving so? Yuh was thinking bout it during the marriage ceremony. Me was thinking bout it too. Only trouble is, what A did expect an what A get was two different things. Is like YOU reach where YOU was going, while I still going up the hill....

JIM: What yuh saying to me? Say dat A don't satisfy yuh?

[*Pause*]

Is five times yuh breed. How yuh mean A don't satisfy yuh?

GLORIA: All A'm saying is dat when yuh gone leave me, A had to carry miself over the hill.

JIM: To rass!

GLORIA: At first A though something was wrong with me ...

TREVOR RHONE   75

JIM: But must....

GLORIA: Yuh see what A mean. Yuh see why A could never talk to yuh 'bout it.

JIM: Say me nuh satisfy yuh. After me all jack yuh up wid twins....

GLORIA: Because A breed, it nuh mean A satisfy....

JIM: Something wrong wid yuh....

GLORIA: Nutten wrong wid me.

JIM: Jesus Christ woman. How many times yuh tell me how yuh enjoy yuhself wid me? So what yuh coming wid now?

GLORIA: A never volunteer the information. Is yuh ask me.

JIM: An what yuh say?

[*The following two speeches are spoken at the same time.*]

GLORIA: A never want to hurt yuh feelings, Jim. If yuh was happy, A was happy. But after a while A say to miself, "But Jim not thinking bout me, him only thinking bout him damn self." So A had to do something for me. An all dem times when yuh was out wid yuh little sweetheart, an come back cock sure o' yuhself an don't need me, I done make certain dat A don't need yuh either.

JIM: How yuh could defile yuhself so? A woman body is her temple, the altar of her shrine. Yuh risk mad house for self gratification!? Yuh hair could o' drop out. Imagine me married to a bald head woman. Nice quiet Gloria! An all the time I think 'bout yuh as the little lady I married. Nice quiet Gloria, mi ass! An all dat shit bout wash plate! A should o' bruck the whole lot o' dem! A going down the road.... A must find somebody NORMAL to deal wid....

GLORIA: A don't understand yuh. Yuh can't manage yuh homework properly, yet yuh taking on extracurricular activity....

JIM: Put it dis way, I can't compete with Niagara Falls!

[*He goes across and throws her picture down.*]

[*JIM exits. GLORIA stops for a moment, then goes to her handbag. She takes out a piece of paper, goes to the phone and dials ll3.*]

GLORIA: Operator. Calling Miami 305-595-5941, to speak to Mr. Johnny Peters the Third. Calling from 92 28461. My name? Mrs. Johnny Peters the Third.

[*BLACKOUT*]

Act II, Scene iii

[*The lights go up on GLORIA packing. A knocking is heard at the front door. GLORIA leaves her packing, looks through the peep hole at the front door to the outside, and sees JIM. In his hurry at the end of the previous scene, he forgot to take his key. She opens the door and leaves immediately for the bedroom area. JIM enters and sits at the dining table.*]

JIM: Gloria ...

GLORIA: What?

JIM: Come here.

GLORIA: For what?

JIM: A want to say something to yuh.

GLORIA: What about?

JIM: A sorry 'bout what happen dis evening.

GLORIA: Me, too.

JIM: A come to a decision.

GLORIA: Me, too.

JIM: Gloria, A going try an deal with it.

GLORIA: Deal with what?

JIM: Yuh an dat thing.

[*GLORIA comes into the dining area.*]

GLORIA: What thing?

JIM: The thing dat cause the friction between us.

GLORIA: There has always been friction between us. The only way dere will ever be peace is if I shut mi mouth, an I done bite mi tongue an swallow mi spit.

JIM: Gloria ...

GLORIA: Dat thing! Yuh can't even bring yuhself to say it! So how yuh going deal with it?

JIM: A go deep into miself, an come to certain realizations. None of us is perfect....

GLORIA: An yuh more perfect than me. In fact, A am the perfect fart.

[*She leaves for the bedroom.*]

JIM: A didn't mean it so....

GLORIA: So how yuh mean it den? 'Bout none of us is perfect?

[*GLORIA goes into the bathroom. JIM follows her to the bedroom. He sees her packing.*]

JIM: What yuh doing? Where yuh going?

[*GLORIA returns from the bathroom and tosses some toilet articles into the suitcase.*]

Is not enough dat A say A will try an deal with it?

GLORIA: No. Is not enough. Yuh can't deal wid something yuh don't understand. Dat yuh not even willing to try an understand. Every time A go bathroom, yuh go wonder is what A up to inside dere. An every time the water bill come, yuh go wonder how it so high....

JIM: Don't bring it up again. A willing to forget it.

GLORIA: Is so yuh planning to deal wid it, by forgetting it?! No, Jim, all it will do is stay under the surface an fester.

JIM: Gloria, A not letting yuh go!

GLORIA: Why not, Jim?

JIM: Yuh belong to me.

GLORIA: A'm not yuh property to lend, lease, or rent. Yuh selfishness in the bed is just the tip of the iceberg. In every other area o' wi life is the same thing. Yuh too damn selfish. An dat is what yuh have to deal with. Yuh selfishness.

JIM: Is not one or two sacrifice A make for yuh an the family? Every farthing A ever earn come into dis house.

GLORIA: Dat is not enough. Every farthing I ever earn come in here too. Money is not the problem. What yuh ever give of yuhself? When yuh ever do something yuh don't want to do, dat will put yuh out of yuh way, enh? Apart from yuh selfishness, yuh is a vindictive an destructive man. Why yuh mash the plates?

JIM: A will buy dem back, Gloria....

GLORIA: They can't replace....

[*She leaves the bedroom to go to the kitchen area to collect the remaining plates. He goes after her.*]

Why Jim? Coz yuh know dem is dear to me. Is a wicked act. Anyhow, it don't matter now. Is years now yuh beat me into submission an try to make me feel dat A not up to much, coz yuh had to feel yuh was General King Kong. Putting me on the plane was the best thing yuh ever do for me. Everytime A come up 'gainst a obstacle, A find a way 'round it.

[*She brushes past JIM as she leaves the dining area and returns to the bedroom.*]

If A can deal with life on an international level, why A should make yuh subject me to be nutten but a damn dishwasher. A finish wid dat — so between now an' when A leave ...

JIM: Gloria, we go through too much together to end up like dis. Think 'bout the children. What about Pops' sacrifice? Yuh can't walk out just so....

GLORIA: Dat idea yuh have 'bout Pops sacrificing himself for the children nutten like dat. When yuh lay down the law dat the children must go up dere, get lost, don't communicate, I discuss it wid Pops. An Pops agree dat we couldn't abandon the children. Read dis —

[*She gives him a letter.*]

Read it.

[*JIM starts to read.*]

JIM: Rub a dub dub, three men in a tub.... What kind o' nonsense is dis?

GLORIA: Is a letter from Suzie. Pops help we work out the code. Dat tell me dat she living with a family an she hoping to do Computer Programming.

JIM: Dis?

GLORIA: Dat! Yuh read Pops wrong. Him knew all along where the children was, an what was happening to dem. Yuh can't use the children or Pops as an excuse any longer....

JIM: A don't understand. Mi old man conspire 'gainst me. If yuh know all dis time, why we go through all the distress, the starvation to get the visa?

GLORIA: A had a dream 'bout America, so when yuh start to see it my way, A jump at the chance. A wanted to see mi children again. A still want to see dem, but as Pops say the night him dead ... "The children going to be alright."

JIM: A worse don't understand.... Pops kill himself for nutten.

GLORIA: No Jim. Him thank me the night for all the years o' looking after him, an then him say "Is time now for you an Jim to look after each other." What Pops do was clear the space so we can deal with each other, an find weself. As long as him was in the house, we would depend on him for everything. America won't solve we problems, whether we go, or whether we stay, until we start to look into weself an learn to help each other. Then we must expect to fail. All dat ever held us together was crisis, Jim. The greater the crisis, the closer we was. The crisis over, Jim. Is yuh an me now. The problem is between us; an A know yuh won't change, an yuh won't compromise. So let me know if yuh still want to go to America. I will get yuh up. A owe yuh dat much. A will get my divorce and A will marry yuh again. It will be a business marriage, so yuh will sign a document agreeing to a divorce....

JIM: And if A don't sign it.

GLORIA: Is up to you, Jim.

[*The lights go down on them.*]

Act II, Scene iv

[*GLORIA is in the bedroom writing a note.*]

GLORIA: "Dear Jim, There is something I didn't have a chance to tell yuh. I hope you don't misunderstand, so I will start at the beginning....

[*She stops, looks up.*]

Where do I begin?

[*JIM enters.*]

JIM: Gloria — you bitch, where yuh is?

[*GLORIA crumples the note.*]

Yuh never hear me calling yuh?

GLORIA: What is it Jim?

JIM: Yuh cunning little bitch!

GLORIA: Let me get outa dis house.

[*She goes to the phone and dials.*]

JIM: You do me dat? YOU woman ... After 20 years ... Jesus God Gloria ... Yuh play me for an ass, a damn ginny ... yuh betray me.... Man kill woman for less!

[*GLORIA speaks into the telephone.*]

GLORIA: Send a taxi for me to ...

[*JIM snatches the phone.*]

JIM: Yuh not leaving till yuh tell me the reason why yuh leaving me.

GLORIA: A tell yuh already.

[*She is going.*]

JIM: Siddown.

GLORIA: Let me leave in peace, nuh man.

JIM: Last night, after A leave the house ...

GLORIA: Oh Jesus ...

JIM: Him can't help yuh now. Only the truth can set yuh free. What yuh do last night after A leave the house? Who yuh call?

[*Pause*]

Who yuh call Gloria?

[*Pause*]

Cat bite yuh tongue bitch!?!

[*She exits to the bedroom.*]

Operator — overseas? Get me Miami — 305-595-5941 ...

GLORIA: Jim ...

[*She comes rushing back.*]

JIM: A want to talk to a Mr. Johnny A Dog Catcher. Yes, Operator, yuh heard right.... Dog Catcher! Dat's the name....

GLORIA: Jim. Please.

JIM: Calling on behalf of his wife, Mrs. Johnny A. Cornflakes Dog Catcher the Third....

GLORIA: Jim, leave him out of it....

JIM: Move bitch! Play me for a ASS — 'bout yuh don't want to go to America ...

GLORIA: It have nutten to do wid him....

JIM: What yuh do last night after A leave the house?

GLORIA: A call the man, Jim.

[*JIM hangs up.*]

GLORIA: A was writing you a letter to explain....

[*She gives him the crumpled note. He takes it, looks at it, tosses it away.*]

JIM: Explain....

[*He produces a tape.*]

I Watergate yuh ass. A tell yuh don't talk on the phone. A have it as dem say — verbatim, word for word.

[*He reels off the tape, speaking pseudo-American.*]

"Gloria mah babes — A was here just dozing off and mah mind was right on yuh. Yuh made mah day, and now to hear yuh call. Yuh make mah night complete...." Yuh want me to go on Gloria?

[*Pause*]

What A tell yuh — A is the General! Yuh believe me now? Don't trifle with the General — Babes...!

GLORIA: I know it look a way, but nothin' happen.

JIM: Yuh lie Gloria. The Yankee man screw yuh.

GLORIA: No ...

JIM: The man take mi 1500 dollar an screw yuh on top o' it....

GLORIA: Him never take the money.

[*Pause*]

JIM: Say what!! Him didn't take the money?!

GLORIA: Jim, let me explain it to yuh.

JIM: What yuh saying to me? What kinda love is dis? So where is the money?

GLORIA: A lodge it in Miami, so we would have a start....

JIM: We? We who?

GLORIA: Me and yuh, Jim.

JIM: Me and yuh? Yuh mean yuh and the Dogcatcher....

GLORIA: No, yuh and me ...

JIM: Bankbook.

[*Holds his hands out for it*]

GLORIA: It in Miami....

JIM: With who?

[*Pause*]

GLORIA: With him ...

JIM: What yuh saying to me? The dogcatcher strikes again....

GLORIA: A couldn't very well bring it back....

JIM: Yuh is a legal U.S. citizen. Yuh don't have to hide. If A never come back today, yuh would be gone an not a word to me.... Half o' dat money is mine.

GLORIA: If A wanted to carry yuh down A wouldn't come back.... What A come back for, to tell yuh A gone again?

JIM: Yuh come back for yuh things. Say yuh don't want to go to America. Yuh mean yuh don't want me to, coz yuh have yuh man up dey....

GLORIA: Jim, yuh don't understand....

JIM: No, A don't understand. Worse, A don't understand how it get to "Gloria, mah Babes."

GLORIA: Jim ... Yuh don't listen to me.... A meet the man.... A say hello, A say I do, an dat was supposed to be dat. It wasn't my choice dat me an the man had to stay

TWO CAN PLAY

together. Is not little cuss A cuss yuh....

JIM: Cuss me?

GLORIA: Yes. A cuss yuh for putting me in dat position where A was completely at the mercy o' the man. A cuss yuh because yuh put *me* out in front to do the dutty work.

JIM: What's dat go' to do wid him calling yuh "Babes"?

GLORIA: A expect the worse an A get the bes'. The man treat me like a lady. Him don't even know me. Him put himself out o' him way to put me at ease, an to help me, an him never expect anything in return. A was suspicious o' the man, A wonder what him want. The only man A had to judge him off was you, an from you who A expect the best, A get the worst!

JIM: Go to yuh man, Gloria, A don't want to hear no more.

GLORIA: You going to listen to me Jim, just like how the man listen to me. Him listen to me an him respect mi opinion, an not once him say A chat nonsense! Yes, Jim, him call me "Babes," because him like me ... but him respect mi wishes, coz A can't deal wid more dan one at a time, so A come back to try an sort it out.

JIM: Nutten to sort out Gloria. Call the taxi, go 'bout yuh business. But before yuh go, dere is a score A have to settle with yuh.

GLORIA: A will get your half o' the money to yuh.

JIM: Is not money I dealing wid. Is *you*. Yuh say I never satisfy yuh ... well A want one more shot.

[*He grabs her, and throws her down on the bed.*]

GLORIA: Jim...!

JIM: Yes Gloria, A deserve a last try, an yuh can scream down the house....

[*JIM pins GLORIA down on the bed with his weight and attempts to undress her and himself at the same time. GLORIA lies motionless and limp on the bed. JIM is turned off by her unresponsiveness. She neither fights nor accepts. He stops, gets off her and turns away defeated.*]

JIM: Is okay, Gloria. Go catch yuh plane....

[*GLORIA sits up on the bed.*]

GLORIA: Jim ...

JIM: The quicker yuh go Gloria, the better.

[*GLORIA gets up off the bed.*]

GLORIA: Jim ...

JIM: Yes.

[*He answers sharply and vehemently.*]

GLORIA: All A wanted was a little reassurance from you. A was longing to see yuh, but the night A come back, all A get was ...

[*She picks up her handbag and turns to leave the bedroom.*]

JIM: A was glad to see yuh, Gloria....

GLORIA: Yuh never show it Jim....

JIM: Is so life go sometimes....

[*JIM is silent. GLORIA turns to go, when JIM again stops her.*]

JIM: A couldn't get out o' the bed Gloria ... because ...

GLORIA: A know, yuh tell me ...

JIM: No. A couldn't get out because ... because ... because A was doing dat t'ing.

GLORIA: What t'ing? Jim?

JIM: Dat t'ing, dat make hair grow in yuh hand middle....

GLORIA: *YOU* Jim!

JIM: Yes Gloria.

GLORIA: But Jim ...

JIM: A know. All evening A was here an A couldn't get yuh out mi mind. A keep looking at yuh picture. A wanted yuh Gloria, and every turn A turn yuh picture was watching me, so A turn it round. Gloria, A going say something A never say to you or admit to miself for twenty years .... A love yuh, Gloria.

[*The telephone rings ... JIM goes into the dining area and answers it.*]

JIM: Hello ... yes ... she here.

[*To GLORIA*]

Overseas for yuh.

GLORIA: Me?

[*JIM throws the phone on the kitchen counter and brushes past her to the bedroom. GLORIA picks it up tentatively.*]

Hello? Yes ... Who is dat? ... Why yuh call me here? Really, for true ... Jim! ... Hold on.... Jim!... Jim!...Jim! Jim, is Paul....

[*He returns.*]

JIM: Paul? Our Paul?

[*She nods.*]

On the phone?

GLORIA: Yes ...

JIM: You mad! Hang it up!

GLORIA: He married to a U.S. citizen....

JIM: Paul?

GLORIA: Talk to him.

JIM: Paul — how yuh do? A'm fine. Yuh mother tell me. Is true? For real?

[*He speaks to GLORIA.*]

Gloria, A don't know what to say.

[*He hands her the phone.*]

GLORIA: Talk...

JIM: Dere's a lot A have to say to yuh son, but ahmm ... kiss the bride for me an, Paul, take care o' yuhself, an don't take her for granted. Work together for the good o' the marriage. Take the advice from a experienced married man. Share wid her, listen to what she have to say. Take it seriously, even if she chatting nonsense. Yuh hear what A say ... an Paul, make certain the two o' yuh go over the hill together.... Is okay. A will explain when A see yuh. Talk to yuh mother....

[*He gives the phone to GLORIA.*]

GLORIA: A will write an tell yuh everything. I love you, too.

[*She says this to JIM. He looks away from her toward the children.*]

Okay mi baby — Bye.

[*She hangs up. They look at each other.*]

JIM: Jus' you an me alone now....

[*A knocking is heard at the front gate. JIM and GLORIA look at each other ... then JIM looks out through the front door peep holes.*]

JIM: Is the man who want to buy the house.

[*Pause*]

GLORIA: Which house? Tell him to go 'bout him business.

[*She picks up her suitcase and returns to the bedroom. She is by the bedroom window.*]

[*JIM speaks quietly.*]

JIM: We not selling....

[*GLORIA looks out the window.*]

GLORIA: Jim ... Jim!

[*JIM goes into the bedroom.*]

Jim...the Orange Tree...it blossoming!

[*JIM goes toward the window and looks out toward the orange tree. JIM is very close on GLORIA. She turns away from the window, and their faces almost touch. The closeness makes JIM uncomfortable. He backs away.*]

JIM: A will move into Pops' room. A plan to court yuh proper dis time. An one ting A promise yuh ...

[*He points to the bed.*]

Not before we married.

[*GLORIA laughs teasingly at JIM.*]

GLORIA: Jim, yuh chatting nonsense. Come here....

[*She lies on the bed.*]

THE END

Scenes from the KET
production of

TWO CAN PLAY

*Starring Grace McGhie
and
Charles Hyatt*